Shattered Dreams

An Alcoholic's Journey

Phil Spencer

WestBow
PRESS
A DIVISION OF THOMAS NELSON

Scripture taken from the New King James Version. Copyright 1979,1980,1982 by Thomas Nelson, Inc. Used by permission. All rights reserved

WestBow Press books may be ordered through booksellers or by contacting:

WestBow Press
A Division of Thomas Nelson
1663 Liberty Drive
Bloomington, IN 47403
www.westbowpress.com
1 (866) 928-1240

ISBN: 978-1-4908-1247-2 (sc)
ISBN: 978-1-4908-1249-6 (hc)
ISBN: 978-1-4908-1248-9 (e)

Library of Congress Control Number: 2013918582

Printed in the United States of America.

WestBow Press rev. date: 10/22/2013

This book is dedicated to the men, women, and children who are struggling with the bondage of pride and rebellion that can lead to alcoholism and drug usage.

Acknowledgments

It had been on my mind for some time to write this book, but meeting a man named Gabor Batizy made me stop being complacent. He lived a life similar to mine but grew up under communism in the eastern block of Europe. He told me how he wanted to put his life down on paper, and I believe God used him to remind me to get this book done.

There is another brother in Christ named Ken Gher who encouraged me to keep going and also advised on how to get it to a point where someone would look at it. I would like to thank both of these men for their support and help.

I sent for my military records years ago, and they gave me the dates and names of units I served with. Also there were the names of the men I served with at different locations throughout the world. It's interesting how God puts things together. I would like to thank the blue-capped crusader who comes to our meetings in the Rehabilitation Center to protect Mike, Don, and myself—or at least that is what she tells the three of us as she munches on crackers. She has a soft spot in her heart for old guys.

I also want to thank my sister, Carol, for the outstanding work she has done on our family's genealogy for the past thirty-five years, supplying me with the dates and names I used.

Preface

This is a project the Lord has wanted me to do for some time. It has been a reminder that I am but a piece of clay, never knowing what the final outcome is going to be because God is not yet finished. But I trust him to do with me as he will, for he is the only one who is capable of changing Phil. I had to go through everything I did to get to where I am today. If one experience had been missing, the outcome to this point would have been different.

I know nothing but what God taught me through other people. They are the ones he used to force me to grow up. I take no credit for my sobriety or for the length of it. I do accept responsibility for the screw-ups I committed—some intentional and some unintentional. I pray you will obtain something from this book to give you a ray of hope. There is a path out of the mess you are sitting in, but you have to want to get out of it. There is no longer an excuse for being there other than what you are sitting in is warm, smells good to you, and is yours, so you enjoy sitting in what you created. I have been to the depths of insanity, so I know what is there. This is not a religious book, but it is a book about the one I have a spiritual relationship with and how he worked in my life to get me sober and continues to keep me sober.

Even though I have written about Vietnam, it is only with regard to the insanity of my drinking and not about my combat experience. This book is as I remember it and how I saw people, places, and things at the time I experienced them.

Chapter 1

The old Methodist church looked the same as I remembered, with thirty-foot ceilings that rose majestically to a peak, old stained-glass windows, and all the beautiful furniture and trappings made out of oak. My great-grandfather Walter Clay Rouse helped build this church and supported it his whole life with the giving of time and money. I was baptized here when I was a baby on the very altar I was now shaking my fist at and sang in the choir here when I was about twelve years old. But my road in life had taken a different turn than most of the people who were in that choir.

This same church sent me a care package when I was a seventeen-year-old kid stationed in Korea. I was surprised and happy to get the package, and then I opened it. On top was a form letter asking me to put five dollars in an envelope and send it back to them to help pay for the package. Won't say what I put in the envelope, but I never received another package from them.

I was standing in the back of the church with fresh snowflakes melting on my shoulders. Outside was a winter scene people dream of, with large snowflakes falling slowly onto the ground. It was one o'clock in the morning, and I had just left the bar at Roeditcher's in Freeland, Michigan.

It was December 1968, and I was home on leave from Vietnam, having already served one year with another six months to go. Walking home that night and past the church brought back a flood of memories. That's when I found myself inside screaming at God, asking him, *Why? Why did you not answer my prayers as I was growing up? Why did you put me in an abusive, alcoholic family to fend for myself? Why did you desert me when I needed you the most?*

The hope of my youth had left a long time ago, and now there was nothing but rage deep within my soul. The life I had lived up to this point was full of fear and chaos, and where the flame of hope had burned out was only deadness. Death did not bother me, and the taking of life did not seem very important. I was what you would consider a lost soul on a fast track to the graveyard.

Both my parents were alcoholics when I was growing up. Mom died from it at the young age of forty-eight when her liver stopped working. She had been committed to the mental institution at Traverse City, Michigan, from time to time, and I still remember the long car rides to visit her. The courts put her in the asylum for a number of reasons. She wrote bad checks while she was drinking, tried killing herself a couple of times, and suffered from a lot of emotional and physical abuse. Mom and Dad had their own demons they struggled with all their adult lives, and some of those same demons I took on later in my life. If you come from a dysfunctional family, that is what you know and create for yourself. If the dysfunction is never treated, it never gets better; it just keeps eating away at you until there is nothing left.

My parents were married on November 10, 1944, in Richmond, North Carolina, when Mom was sixteen years old and Dad was twenty-one. They were planning to be married when Dad was home on leave from Europe, but there was an argument between their mothers, so they called off the wedding, and Dad headed to Fort Bragg, North Carolina. Mom had become pregnant when Dad was home on leave, so two months later, she took a bus from Freeland, Michigan, to North Carolina, and they were married. This was during WWII, when lots of crazy things were going on, and no one knew if their husbands, sons, brothers, or daughters were going to return from the battlefield.

Dad had already been to Europe and was now taking airborne glider assault training at Fort Bragg. The time came for him to ship out to the Philippines, with Mom going back to Freeland to live on Grandma and Grandpa Spencer's farm. It was a small family farm of about sixty acres, as Grandpa also worked for the railroad.

My brother, Butch, was born in the spring of 1945, and he and Mom moved into the milk house, a small building measuring about twenty-four feet long and twelve feet wide. A potbelly stove heated it in the winter. I don't know why they didn't stay with Mom's parents. It probably would have been better if they had because Grandma Spencer was always sticking her nose where it didn't belong. There was no love lost between my mom and grandma. I believe they disliked each other until the day they died.

After a lot of arguing between Mom and Grandma, Grandma took Butch into the main farmhouse, and that was that. Mom was seventeen years old at the time and was probably intimidated by Grandma. But that also freed her up to do what normal seventeen-year-old girls do. Some people from that time believe Grandma took Butch into her house to replace her son, Leon, who had died of injuries from a car accident on August 17, 1943.

Grandma was an arrogant, overbearing woman who became extremely abusive when she didn't get her way. I didn't realize many things about her until I was older. I lived with my grandparents for a while after I was discharged from the army, and it was amazing how Grandma tried to control my life. But that stopped the first time I had a flashback about Vietnam while I was drinking.

I had closed the bar that night. Just as I walked into my grandparents' house, I was back in Vietnam, and the VC was overrunning us. I remember yelling, "Kill them all before they get too far inside the wire!" Explosions were going off, and there was mayhem everywhere. I clawed my way up the wall, swearing because I couldn't find my rifle. It was as real as if I were there. As I was coming out of it, I remember seeing my grandparents standing there with Grandpa holding a baseball bat, ready to swing. I think that was when Grandma realized just how unstable I had become.

Grandma liked to sit in her favorite rocking chair reading the big family Bible and always left it beside the chair for everyone to see. The only problem was there was no fruit of the Spirit in her life. I believe the Bible was another one of her props to draw people to her way of thinking. She had a lot of religion but very little, if any, spirituality.

Grandpa died on June 25, 1975, from stomach cancer when he was seventy-two years old. The first time he went into the hospital, Grandma visited him. But the second time he went in, she told him as he was leaving the house that she was not going with him and would not visit him, using the excuse that she could not stand hospitals. Maybe that was the reason, or maybe she didn't want to watch him die. Who knows? But Grandpa never saw her again after he left the house that night. I wonder what he thought as he laid there in pain from a cancerous tumor the size of a football in his stomach, knowing he was dying and his wife of fifty-four years refused to be with him as he passed on.

Grandpa could be a hard man, but he had a soft spot for people. He brought home what they called bums who rode the railroad cars and gave them a place to stay for a few days while trying to find them work. He had quit his heavy drinking before I was born, and I only knew him to drink a beer once in a while. He worked for fifty-four years at the railroad, starting out as a water boy at the age of fourteen and finishing his career as a section foreman.

A Methodist pastor came to see Grandpa as he lay in the hospital bed and told him about the love of Jesus. Grandpa crossed into eternity trusting the Lord, and I believe I will see him again when I cross over. But I have my doubts about Grandma. The only time she backed off was when Grandpa referred to her as "woman," for then she knew she had crossed the line. I don't know how Grandpa put up with her for all the years they were married. I guess he loved her in spite of what she had become.

Chapter 2

After Grandpa died, Dad went to Freeland to take care of his mother at all hours of the day and night. He had promised Grandpa he would, and that's what he did. I believe Grandma took advantage of Dad, using his promise as an excuse to pay him back for the wrongs she thought he had done to her over the years. I don't believe she liked Dad all that much, as her actions on more than one occasion showed.

Dow Chemical Company, where Dad worked, went on strike, and the old man was hurting for money, so he used Grandma's gas card and borrowed money from her until he got back to work. According to him, he paid it all back, but she always held it over his head, telling people what she had done for him. She liked having people indebted to her and used it against them when she thought it would benefit her or make them look bad. Grandma moved in with her oldest daughter at the very end of her life because she no longer could take care of herself.

My sister, Carol, was eleven months younger than me and was born in early 1948. She thinks something terrible must have happened in Grandma's childhood to make her act like she did. I know she lost her first child—a daughter—at birth, and then Leon, her son, was in a car accident on his eighteenth birthday and died shortly after.

I don't think her attitude had anything to do with his death, though, cause he was moving out because of the relationship between him and his mother. She tried to control his life, and he would have none of it.

She blamed Dad for his death because he had allowed Leon to use his car while Dad was in the military. They thought he was speeding and that caused the accident, but in the end they found out the tie-rod had broken. I believe Grandma acted the way she did because that was her character. Grandpa Spencer's mother (Hattie Spencer) didn't like Grandma Spencer and even went so far as not setting a place for her at the table when Grandma Hattie would invite them over for dinner. I used to think Dad might have been different if Leon had lived, but I realize now that even if his brother had lived, it would not have changed anything. The old man had too many demons to deal with that he didn't even know he had.

When Dad came home from the war, he took Butch back from Grandma, moving into the milk house with Mom. They lived there until they built a house about three-quarters of a mile east of the farm. This was the house the three of us kids spent most of our childhood in. There were a few other houses around us but not many.

When Grandma Spencer died on June 28, 1985, at the age of eighty-one, Dad was given a letter in which Grandma left him two pennies and a note saying that was all he was getting. I never understood the anger Dad had toward Grandma and others until I found out about the letter after Dad died. The hurt, pain, and anguish the letter inflicted on him became almost more than he could bear. Like I said, she had to have the last word. It was a spiteful thing to do to anyone, let alone your only son, but that is the way she was.

Looking back I believe Mom and Dad had a love-hate relationship that was fueled ever so often by Grandma Spencer sticking her nose into their marriage. Their marriage started like a lot of marriages did during that time period. It was a quick marriage because of a child soon to be born followed by long separations because of the war while Mom was at home with a small child.

I have read letters Dad sent to Grandma Spencer while he was in the Philippines ranting and raving about what Mom was doing. How could a man seven thousand miles away know what his teenage wife was doing back home? All of the letters where he spoke about this were sent to Grandma. It's hard to say what kind of letters he was receiving or from whom, but it sure fired him up.

Dad saw heavy combat while he was in the Philippines, and he carried that with him the rest of his life. I doubt if he knew combat fatigue—as they called it back then—was even a part of his temperament. Knowing the way alcohol makes you think, I can say without question he thought all of his problems were from outside sources.

Mom wasn't an angel while he was gone or even during the marriage. I found this out because of the research my sister has done. It was the brewing of a perfect storm with three small children caught in the middle. There were times when we had what could be called a normal family, but there was always drinking involved no matter where we were. The further along in the marriage, the more the alcohol became a priority. I hated the weekends, which started on Thursday nights (payday) and went to Sunday. You never knew what was going to take place or what kind of insanity was going to happen.

Chapter 3

There was a rumor that Dad gave Butch and me beer in our baby bottles to get us to sleep when Mom wasn't around. I don't know how true it was, but when we ask him later, he never denied it. When I was about eight or nine years old, I started to take sips from people's beer when they weren't looking, and when I got the chance, I would steal a bottle to take outside and drink. I liked how it made me feel, and my problems seemed to evaporate into thin air. Life was better, and I felt like I fit in when I drank the little I did, but that would not last forever. The three of us kids knew it was not a good idea to invite anyone over when Mom and Dad were drinking. If we did have someone sleep over, we pitched a tent as far from the house as we could so we wouldn't hear them fighting when they came home drunk.

Sometimes the neighborhood kids would try to understand, but other times they would make fun of what took place. This only caused us more heartache and gave us a feeling of greater alienation. As children we always wanted the acceptance of those we considered our friends, but that was not always the way it was. All people want to think they have someone to cover their backs, but in most cases they don't.

There were two people in our neighborhood that consistently had my back. One was about five years older and the other was two years older, but whenever push came to shove, they were there. Those two guys were Bob Davy and Jack Graves. One time Jack and I got into an argument, and I used a homemade whip on him. If he had caught me, I probably would have ended up in the hospital. I was scared to go anywhere for weeks, and then one day Jack came around the corner. He drilled me once in the shoulder (still hurts), and that was it. Later on the day I was kicked out of school, it was Jack who stepped in, stopping this guy from ripping me a new one.

Let's face it: all people have self-worth issues, and that includes kids. Back and forth it goes: I'm the toughest, my dad can beat your dad, my house is better, and on and on it goes. There were two kids from the neighborhood who stood outside our house one day chanting, "Rats ran in, rats ran out, rats ran all over Spencer's house." The sad part was it was true. There were more mice than you could shake a stick at, and every so often we would see a rat in the house. I was about nine or ten years old at the time. It's amazing how more than fifty-five years later I still remember. The cruelty of children can never be overstated.

I remember well the guys from my old neighborhood. It was a fairly tight group of kids, but we could get on each other's nerves and then there would be mayhem for a while. We had a neighborhood bully, and this guy was always in trouble for something. I never knew him to be any other way, and they tell me he was the same for years after I left the neighborhood. My sister sent me his obituary a few years back, and I have often wondered if he found Jesus.

Bob Davy and Buddy Webster were in the military as well, and out of this group of guys as far as I know I was the only one to experience combat. I don't believe any of the other neighborhood guys served in the military because they went to college or got married. I understand Bob Webster and Gary Graves kept in contact, remaining close over the years. People think they will be buddies forever with the people they grow up with, but that very seldom happens. When I came back from Vietnam, we had nothing in common even though at the time I thought we did.

As I said, my parents had a love-hate relationship. The fighting became worse as the marriage progressed. I would stay awake at night when they went out to the bars. At the sound of car wheels crunching on the gravel in the driveway, I would run for the bedroom, pulling the sheets over my head and hoping to block out what I knew was coming. It was a rotten way for small children to live.

The fighting usually did not start right away, but eventually something would set them off. Carol recalls nights when Dad would choke Mom, slamming her head against the floor. One time Carol picked up a butcher knife, threatening to stab him if he didn't stop. Then there would be fistfights, with both sides throwing punches or anything they could get their hands on. Mom hit Dad once with a skillet, and he dropped like a rock. You never knew if someone was going to die during these battles. Children should not have to watch the two people they love the most trying to kill each other right before their eyes. Society wonders why kids are so full of anger, pain, and confusion. There was an instance when Dad was trying to stop her from leaving with the car, and he reached inside to shut it off. She dragged him down the road about 150 feet before he let go. It's a wonder he didn't roll underneath the car. I still have a picture of that in my mind.

We had been given a big boxer bulldog named Buster, and Buster did not like fighting or loud voices. They came home one night drunk, fighting, and yelling. Buster put one in a corner and the other one in another corner, and that's where they stayed all night. Unfortunately, that was the end of Buster. He was gone the next day. When he left, it was like my only protector had been taken away, and I was all alone again. I sure did love that dog.

Butch and I did something that ticked off the old man when I was about ten years old, so out to the garage we went for the usual whipping. Instead of the belt, though, he picked up a piece of board that was laying there. He either didn't know or else didn't care that there were nails sticking out of it. It must have made an impression because I never forgot it.

The old man's favorite move was to backhand or smack you in the back of the head, and he did both of them quite often. I didn't believe in or understand the word love when I was growing up. It was a word some people used, but I knew it did not apply to me. I was awed by the kids at school who would tell me what they had done as a family that weekend and how their parents had done such and such with them. There were some kids and parents who liked to look down on kids like me. It would have been nice to have had them around as extra sandbags when crap was hitting the fan in 'Nam.

Chapter 4

Christmas Eve was always a time of chaos because my parents never came home from work without stopping at the bar first. They would arrange it so Mom had to pick Dad up from work. We would feel the joy and excitement all kids feel on Christmas Eve. However, then reality would set in that they weren't coming home, and when they did, it wasn't going to be joyful, although there would be excitement.

One year Dad threw the Christmas tree out the front door, and it stayed there until the next morning—another thing for the neighbor's to see. Sometimes we got wrapped presents, and sometimes we didn't. In another drunken episode, Mom tried to kill herself by putting a belt around her neck and pulling it so tight she turned blue with her eyes starting to bulge out. Somehow she latched it and was lying on the floor in the bathroom between the sink and commode. We yelled for Dad, and he was able to cut the belt off before she died. She went to Traverse City, a mental institution, over that one. While she was committed, she received a number of shock treatments because they thought back then that was the way to fix everything. How can putting a sudden electrical shock through a person's brain help her? Mankind is stupid with his superior knowledge.

I was walking with some of the neighborhood kids in town one day and saw the police were ripping apart our car in front of one of the bars. I found out later they were looking for heroin they believed Mom was bringing back from her Chicago trips. Toward the end of their marriage, Mom would take off a couple of times a year. Then she would come back, and everything would be, "We love each other so much," but we kids knew it would not last and never gave it any credence. Alcohol would always keep coming back to destroy even more than it already had. Alcohol is very patient and will wait in the background for as long as it has to, and then it will raise its ugly head and strike.

Dow Chemical sent Dad to Brighton Rehabilitation a couple of times. If he hadn't gone, he would have lost his job. Mom was treated for everything but alcohol, as I remember, yet she did get sober on a couple of occasions. But they could never stay sober because no one ever treated the real problem, which was their thinking. Alcoholism is the end result of the real problem. They say that it is 10 percent drinking and 90 percent thinking.

While I was in Mrs. Keenan's fourth-grade class, I got into trouble when I went nuts, calling her every name I could think of and throwing everything I could get my hands on. It took a few people grabbing me to get me to quiet down that day. The assistant principal, Mr. Fox, a full-blooded Blackhawk Indian who terrified everyone, had me stand in front of the class and apologize for what I did, both to the class and to Mrs. Keenan. I actually liked Mrs. Keenan, but sometimes you just have to let it all out.

The only time the old man came to one of my Little League games, he left with someone to go to the bar before I got into the game. I was so proud that he had come, and then he left. I was about eleven years old when this happened, and from that point forward, I didn't want either my Dad or Mom at anything I was part of. I believe it was around the same time I started to withdraw, building my walls of protection.

The folks sold the house when I was thirteen years old. That was a time of chaos, with constant drinking and fighting between them. They must have been the toast of the bars, for they never bought another house, and when the money ran out, they were no longer together. As long as you have money, you will always have friends in a bar. We used to wait until they passed out and then divide what money was left in their pockets. I never saw anything wrong with it because of the misery they put us through. I'm not sure how much money we took, but I did get a new catcher's mitt out of it.

When my parents split up, Mom went to Saginaw while Dad moved us to a house in town he rented from Miles Heffel. Miles had a daughter my age named Suzanne who was one of the nicest people I knew. She always left her test papers arranged on her desk so I could see them. If it hadn't been for her, I would have probably spent two years in the third grade. When I was in Vietnam, I received the Midland newspaper that said she had been killed in a car accident shortly after graduating from nursing school. After getting over the shock, I thought, *What is this all about?* It made no sense to me that she was taken and what I considered trash like me would be left. Where was the justice, and where was God? I talked to Miles in a bar

15

years later, and you could tell he never got over Suzanne's death.

We lived in that house until I was fifteen years old. The old man was drinking most nights, and I was running the streets. It is amazing that through all this, Carol was the only one who never got into trouble and the only one to graduate from high school. Carol and I lived with Dad because Butch had moved to Grandma and Grandpa Spencer's house when Mom threw him out several years earlier. I still recall all his clothes lying in the driveway with Mom screaming at him that if he loved the old bag more than her then he should move there. I helped him carry his stuff to Grandma and Grandpa's Spencer's that day. I don't believe Butch ever got over being kicked out of the house by his mother. What kid would?

In the summers I would hitchhike to Coleman, Michigan, staying with Mom's older sister Clistie and her family. Back then you could hitchhike and not have to worry much about it. There was only one time when someone didn't want to let me out, so I called him every name in the book, threatening to punch him out if he didn't stop the car. He finally stopped about a mile beyond where I wanted to get off. The guy was drunk, so what did I expect? I would have been between twelve to fourteen years old at the time.

Aunt Clistie's youngest son, Lonnie, and I were about the same age, so we had stuff in common. We also liked to get in trouble together, and that always worried Grandma Brewster, who was my mom's mother. Aunt Clistie had nine children, and other than Lonnie, my favorite was Karen, one of the twins. She was like a big sister who always looked out for me. Lonnie and I were smoking by then, and she would give us cigarettes when we ran out. When she didn't have any to give us, I would steal them from stores.

One time Lonnie and I put some rifle bullets in a vise, and taking a punch and hammer, we started to fire them off. They sure ricocheted around that cement block garage. We must have gotten five or six fired off before everyone come a-running. Needless to say, we got our butts handed to us that day.

Another time there were six of us in a hollowed-out earthen mound when a cow fell through the roof. Those were some good times because I was away from the chaos in Freeland. I would stay there until I wore out my welcome and then head someplace else. Just think about that—a thirteen—to fourteen-year-old boy hitchhiking all over the state and no one caring anything about it. The insanity of a dysfunctional family has no boundaries.

Dick, another cousin of mine who was my parents' age, had a place on some lake up north. I went there with Lonnie, doing what kids do at lakes. I had been there about two weeks when I heard Dick and Aunt Clistie talking about me staying there and Dick not having enough money to feed everyone who was there. I was on the road a half hour later, with my mind spinning about why I had to live the way I did. The so-called normal kids didn't live like I did because they had parents who cared about them. What had I done to deserve this? I must have done something, and this was God's way of getting back at me.

It is normal for kids to think they are the cause of the trouble going on around them. If only I had done things differently, there wouldn't have been a divorce, my family would still be together, and on and on. It is a heavy load for a young person to be carrying. I heard later that Dick stopped his drinking, asked Jesus in to his life, and moved to Florida. Fifty years later I ran into Karen's twin sister, Sharon, while I was visiting Midland, Michigan. She asked if I remembered coming to her mother's house after getting home from Vietnam and I told her no. She said I was so drunk that day and she had prayed for me every day since. You never know who God will raise up to intercede for you. She was also surprised at how much trouble Lonnie and I got into.

Chapter 5

I look back at the boyhood dreams I had, and there were many. I wanted to be a lawyer when I grew up, but you have to finish the eleventh grade before you can go to college. I wanted to contribute to society, not live on the fringes as I did. I dreamed of a normal family setting with parents who were there every night to protect you and make sure the boogie man wasn't under the bed. It was about growing up and having a family that was respected within the community, with everyone being cared about and loved.

I had the normal dreams and aspirations of youth, thinking I would be able to attain them. No one says that they want to grow up to become an alcoholic or drug addict, but when you are continuously told you are worthless and will never amount to anything, it starts to become reality. After a while, you are beat down, recognizing your dreams are not attainable because your life is a lie and always will be. It doesn't come all at once but slides up on you a moment at a time, a day at a time, until it overwhelms you.

I was thirteen when I accepted life was not going to be the way I hoped it would be. I did not know how it would turn out, and the sad part was I was beginning to not care. There were a bunch of people in the family and our town who thought Carol would get pregnant (which she did not) and I would eventually go to prison. I did go to jail a few times in Korea and France, but I never did do any prison time. We'll talk later about that one.

Chapter 6

Carol and I bounced around before we finally settled into one place. The old man would take off, and we would have to find someplace to stay while he was gone. This would have been between the time my parents sold the house and the old man left for good. We stayed for a time with Grandma Brewster on her farm. Carol and I would walk the railroad tracks between Freeland and her house on different occasions. It was probably a five-mile walk, and I always tried to bust the insulators on the telegraph lines with rocks while we were walking. I would regret that later in life when I was a lineman at the telephone company because of the number of insulators I had to replace because of some stupid kid throwing rocks.

Grandpa and Grandma Brewster were married on February 13, 1906, and were married for thirty-six years. Grandpa was a farmer and the sexton at the Pine Grove Cemetery just outside Freeland, Michigan, during which time he dug the graves for three of his grandchildren. Grandpa Brewster, from what I have been told by people who knew him, was a very nice man.

Dad told me about the time Grandpa walked into town for a beer and stayed a little too long, getting drunk. Somehow Dad got called to bring him home, and from what Dad said, Grandpa laughed all the way home until Grandma met him at the door. Grandpa died when he was fifty-eight years old from stomach cancer. Mom told me the cancer ate through his back and he lived with an open, draining wound until the day he died. This must have been extremely painful for him. Marion, the youngest daughter, would re-pack the wound every day because Grandma was not emotionally able to do it. Grandma would have been fifty-three years old when Grandpa passed.

I understand there was a man who wanted to marry Grandma later in life. She wanted to marry him also but first asked her nine children about it, with one of her sons saying he would disown her if she remarried. She didn't marry the man because of one stupid son. The life she led afterward was not what Grandpa would have wanted for her. He would not have wanted his widow to live her remaining thirty-one years by herself, struggling to make ends meet. The man who wanted to marry her was well-to-do and would have taken good care of Grandma. I would have told the son to kiss off. This son sat in the church pew every Sunday, showing everyone in town he wasn't like some of his brothers and sisters who drank all the time. He always was a strange duck. I wish I would have known this when he was alive because it would have been nice to have had a long talk with him. I wonder what part of honor thy mother and father he didn't understand.

When we were staying with Grandma Brewster, it was either at her farm or where she was a housekeeper for the Lincoln family. Aunt Lola, her husband, John, and their boy, Jimmie, also stayed at Grandma's. It was a real tight fit because she only had two bedrooms in a small farmhouse. Carol would sleep with her, and I slept on the couch. I still remember the porcelain pot at the end of her bed that we would use during the middle of the night instead of going to the outhouse. I always worried about tipping it over on myself when I used it.

One night I heard Aunt Lola, Uncle John, and Grandma talking about where the money was going to come from for the two extra mouths to feed. I helped the best I could around the farm and often went into work with Uncle John. He was a milkman for the Borden Milk Company, and they let me ride on his routes with him. John and Lola were good people, and I have nothing but respect for them.

It is no wonder that today's kid's do what they do with feelings of desertion, loss, and low self-worth or why they go into gangs searching for somewhere to belong. The only thing Carol and I wanted was a place to call home and people to tell us they cared about us. Grandma Brewster loved us but was unable to take care of us, and why should she have had to? Carol and I have always agreed that it was Grandma Brewster who showed her love with action.

Before she died, she made a point of going to the Log Cabin bar in Freeland where members of her family would go to drink. When she walked in the door, the place went silent as they watched her walk to the bar. Everyone in there knew who she was. She ordered a glass of beer, took a sip, set the glass down, and walked out. When asked later why she did it, her reply was that she had always wondered what her kids saw in going to a place like that. She would have been in her mid-seventies at the time. She lived with Mom and Duane for a number of years during some of their worst drinking. Grandma passed on January

14, 1973, at the age of eighty-four with Mary Ellen Cady, one of her granddaughters, holding her hand.

I prayed and prayed to God, but it was like he had a deaf ear when it came to me. I wondered what I had done to deserve what I saw as punishment from God for what was happening in my life. I knew I must have done something terrible because it seemed life kept getting worse.

Where were the good religious people my aunts and uncles were always talking about? Not all of Grandma Brewster's children claimed to be religious, but enough of them did that you would have thought someone would have stepped in to stop the insanity Carol and I were living in. All it would have taken was a call to the courts, and we would have been out of there. But no one called!

I can't say anything about the Spencer side as far as aunts and uncles because they lived in Pennsylvania and could not have cared less about what was happening in Michigan. Uncle John was able to get my cousins out of the mess they were living in with their dad on the Brewster farm. They lived in a very small trailer house across the driveway from the farm house. Before living there, they lived on the other side of the farm in a small four-room house. This all happened after Carol and I had moved back to Freeland. When I talked to my cousin later, she told me she would always be grateful to Uncle John for reporting her dad to social services. They were immediately taken out of the trailer they lived in and placed in foster care. Their dad later died in a one-room flat in Saginaw. It was over a week before they found him so they must have poured him into the body bag.

When I was fifteen years old, I came home from school and Carol was sitting on the front porch of where we lived.

I asked her why she was sitting outside, and she said the door was locked and to look inside the house. When I looked in the window, all the furniture was gone. Carol said the old man had left to do whatever and we were left behind.

She actually remembers this better than I do. She said we sat there until Miles Heffel showed up to check the place over. He found us and called the cops. Then we went to live at Grandma and Grandpa Spencer's. I believe the only reason they took us in was because they were worried about what people in the town would say. Grandma told anyone who would listen how she had to take in laundry and do ironing to help pay for us to stay there. The thing she forgot to tell them was that it was Carol who did the laundry and ironing.

I stayed there on and off for the next year and a half. Carol slept on the couch, with Butch and me sharing a bed in the back bedroom. I was not unique in how I lived. I was just a kid trying to understand why it was the way it was. I knew there were kids in my class who lived in worse conditions than I did. But you know; it is hard to feel sorry for the guy who lost his leg when you have a sliver in your finger.

By then I was on my way to having a problem with alcohol. It's interesting that the one thing I thought I would never become I was heading toward. I really didn't like staying with my grandparents and took every chance I could to stay away. There was a friend of my brother's named Denny who lived in the woods about four miles outside of Freeland. His parents had no problem with me crashing there for a few days on and off, so I moved in as often as I could. I had learned by then not to wear out my welcome, so I would go back to the grandparents' house every once in a while so no one got upset. Denny liked to party, so it seemed like a good fit.

There was a girl named Miki who came to Woodman's during the summer and on weekends. We started to hang out. One thing led to another, and soon we were more than friends. I soon realized she was out of my league because her family had more money than they knew what to do with and she had everything she could want. Here I was a future alky with no car, decent clothes, or anything else that I thought mattered at the time.

I doubt if she understood the reasons why I walked away, but they made sense to me. The last time I saw her was at the Freeland Diner where Denny was working. As I walked out the door, I looked back at her, thinking I had to be nuts. What it came down to was I didn't want to be embarrassed in the future when I knew I would not measure up to what I perceived her standards were. She was a sweet girl, and I hope she found the happiness she deserves.

Denny planned a party for a weekend when his parents were to be gone. Someone called Uncle Don Andrews, a DJ from Saginaw, and he broadcast it over the radio. I could not believe the amount of people who showed up. They were coming out of the woodwork, and it stayed that way from Friday night through Sunday afternoon. On Sunday the empty beer cases were counted, and there were more than eighty. Most people liked Denny, but I remember one guy who was always trying to get him to take a swing. Denny was not a fighter, though, and the guy never got his wish. I tracked him down when I was sixty-four years old, asking him what he had been doing all these years, and he said he was waiting to die. I hope it was only a joke because that is a long time to wait for the inevitable.

Denny and I went to a wedding at the Dice Township Hall one Saturday night, and Carol Leaman from high school was there. I remember sitting on a table with her, talking about anything and everything. It was nice to be accepted at what I perceived to be her level in life. For some reason, we got to talking about my drinking and getting into trouble. I ask her if she would ever have thought of going out with someone like me and she said yes but first I would have to do something about the drinking. Needless to say, we never went out. Even a teenage girl could see I was heading down a dead-end street at a high rate of speed.

I met her forty-five years later at a reunion, and she looked the same as when we had sat on that table so long ago. She asked how it was that she remembered me after all these years when the guy standing next to her didn't. Before I could reply, someone came up and changed the subject. If you ever read this, it was because I got in your space on more than one occasion, and even the last time we saw one another, it seemed that you got upset with me. You care about people, and I happened to be one you cared about even though I didn't live up to your expectations. You accepted me where I was, but you also saw what I could become. Am I a Christian who has sat in church all his life? No, but I'm a long way from that kid sitting on the table next to you at the wedding reception. The Spirit of God starts the change from the inside, but sometimes he leaves the outside rough so we can go where others either can't or won't.

Chapter 7

I have no idea why, but the only class in school I tried to succeed at was typing. Later in life I would use this skill more than any other I learned while in school. I would go to school from Woodman's when I even bothered to go to school because no one seemed to care where I was staying or what I was doing. There were nights when I would stay at either this all-night gas station or a restaurant in town. I didn't want to sleep under the bridge so a window seat or booth was good.

The people in charge of the school and I were not getting along very well, and it seemed as if I was always in someone's office. Denny and I did something that got us in trouble so the powers that be had us write the US Constitution with all the amendments in longhand. I guess it was supposed to be some sort of punishment. It took a couple of weeks to finish, and then they put a punch hole in the middle of it. I don't know what that was supposed to teach us, but at least it kept me out of trouble in the classroom.

Looking back I feel sorry for the teachers because they tried their best to get me interested in classes. No one understood that what they were dealing with was someone with a whole lot of baggage who used alcohol to escape his reality. They were living normal lives while I was trying to survive mine. The easiest way to solve the problem was to get rid of the problem. They didn't have a clue where I was coming from, and I sure didn't understand them.

I do remember the superintendent pulling me into his office with some other people present asking me if I thought I would eventually end up in the Traverse City Insane Asylum like my mother. It actually shocked me that he asked such a question, and I wasn't an easy person to shock. Don't get me wrong, I believe in education. Both of my children have graduate degrees, with one of them being a high school guidance counselor. However, I also believe there is a difference between education and common sense. That superintendent might have had an education, but he didn't have a lick of common sense.

One night Denny and I stopped by the school after it was over, sitting in his car, drinking beer, and watching the track team practice. The track coach, Dan Craig, came over and started to talk to us about getting involved with sports or something that would make us want to come to school more. (By the way, Denny graduated, but I didn't.) I told Mr. Craig that I could outrun the miler on his track team, and he took me up on it. So there we were with the kid who ran the mile in full track uniform and me in street clothes and tennis shoes. We took off, and on the final leg, he was ahead of me by a couple of steps. I have to admit that I cheated by passing him on the inside, but in the end, I was about five yards ahead when we crossed the finish line.

Years later I was sitting at a bar in Freeland when this guy started to tell the story how this drunk beat Mr.

Craig's mile runner in a race. I guess he liked to tell it to his tracks teams. I kept my mouth shut and enjoyed to story. When I was fifty-five years old, I called Mr. Craig to tell him what an impact he had on my life. I thanked him for caring and wished him well. He informed me that I was the only one in his teaching career who had ever told him that. It's a shame that more students haven't because he was a very good teacher and cared about his students.

I made it to the beginning of my junior year, and then the bottom fell out. They told me it would be better if the school district and I parted ways. I was getting into trouble everywhere I went with my drinking and fighting. I had words with one guy who happened to have his hall locker next to mine. The basketball coach had allowed me back onto the team after I was suspended from school, and the night before this guy and I had either gotten into a fight or a shoving match after practice. I can't remember, but I do know I was on my way out the door for good the next morning.

There we were at our lockers at the same time, with him getting books to go to his next class and me cleaning out mine. I didn't figure I had anything to lose, so when he bent over to get a book out of the bottom of his locker, I kicked the door shut on his head. Needless to say, he didn't fare too well from that and was taken to the office.

Then Jack Graves came in, saving my scrawny butt. The guy's older brother wanted a piece of me, and he weighed around 230 pounds to my 117 pounds. As he rounded the corner coming for me, Jack got between us, telling the guy he would have to go through him first. The guy knew Jack was serious and backed away so I was able to leave without getting my butt handed to me.

Only a couple of months before this, the superintendent had kicked me out and my grandparents had gotten me back in, and now I was kicked out again. When I left the school grounds that day, I was in a rage worse than any I had ever experienced up to that point in my life. It was another example to me of how I not only didn't fit in, but I was also stupid for not being able to finish school. How did I think I was going to finish school if I didn't go? I can see where kids today do really senseless things. I'm not saying they're right; I'm just saying I understand. Rage is a very raw and powerful emotion to be caught up in, but little did I know the rage I would experience later in life would make this look like a cakewalk. When I was stationed in Korea, the captain made sure I got a GED certificate. I didn't want to do it, but a private first class doesn't argue with the captain of his company.

After getting thrown out of school, I did odd jobs to get money for cigarettes and beer, but they were not anything to write home about. I did know I would have to start paying for room and board at my grandparents' house if I wasn't in school. Looking back I'm not really sure what took place between the time I was kicked out of school and the time I left Freeland. It's kind of a haze that will not come into focus. I was not a happy camper and blamed everyone for what had happened to me, not wanting to take responsibility for any of my actions. There was lots of drinking and fighting, and I knew deep inside I would eventually go to jail if something didn't change. There definitely was not a Kodak moment during this time of my life.

I remember sitting on the front porch at my grandparents' house with Carol when the old man pulled in with some women I had never seen before. I glanced at Carol, asking her who he was with, and she stated it was his latest girlfriend. Her name was Barb, and the old man was supposedly living with her. That was the first and only time I saw her until I came back from Korea. It's astonishing the things that go on around you and you never notice them when you are caught up in yourself. She would later become a thorn in our side when it came to the old man's relationship between him and his first three children. Dad and Barb found letters when they cleaned out Grandma Spencer's house that had been sent to him from Mom, which she sent to Grandma to give to him, that stated she would like to try to work things out and get back together. Neither of them was married at the time so it might have happened, but needless to say, Grandma never gave the letters to the old man.

When I turned seventeen, the old man informed me I had better join the military before I ended up in jail, prison or dead. I had nothing else going for me, so down to the army recruiter I went. After I took some test, he said I could enlist but had to have both parents' signatures because I wasn't eighteen. The old man went searching the bars in Saginaw, Michigan, to find my mother. After he found her, she promised to go to the recruiters and sign the papers. I got a phone call a few days later telling me she had signed them and when I should report to catch a bus to Detroit for a physical and then be sworn in.

I got to the bus station on time, picked up my papers, and got on the bus. As I looked out the window, I saw the old man standing there with Carol and Grandma. I don't remember if Mom was there or not. Dad told me to go into the combat engineers because there would always be work for me when and if I got out. After I took a test, the recruiter told me I would be going into communications. I didn't have a clue what communications was, but forty-three years later I retired from AT&T.

It was weird because there were tears streaming down the old man's face, which I have often wondered about. Maybe it was love or regret; I don't know. I do know that if I had not gone into the army, I most certainly would have screwed around until I ended up in jail and eventually prison. The kids at school were taking exams, applying to different colleges, and wondering what they were going to do over the summer. I, on the other hand, was heading for an adventure I could not even imagine. It was as if a weight had been lifted off my shoulders. The five years, two months, and twenty-two days I spent in this man's army defined me as a person for the rest of my life, with some of it being good and some bad.

Chapter 8

I arrived at the induction center in Detroit, Michigan, on April 13, 1964, and went through the medical exams. It took the better part of a day, so we were put up overnight at the center. There must have been seventy guys in the bay I was assigned to. During the night you could hear guys crying with others making fun of them and still others telling them to shut up. I couldn't figure out what they would be crying about because I was glad to be leaving. It is hard to explain the emotions I was going through at the time, but I believed that even though I had not a clue as to what was going to happen, I had made the right choice.

The next morning they took about twenty-five of us into a big room, and we were sworn into the US Army for a period of three years. I remember how proud I felt in that I was actually doing something positive with my life for a change even though I didn't know exactly what that was. Seven of us left on a bus later that day for Ft. Knox, Kentucky, with orders to report no later than 2400 hours. We were all new privates E-1 in the army except for Rasmussen, who was in charge of us; he was a private E-2 (prior service).

I remember we got there late at night and a sergeant came onto the bus explaining how it was going to be when we left the bus. He said we had better listen to instructions or our sorry butts would wish we had. This was in the day when they did what they wanted with you and no one cared. As he stepped off the bus, they started to yell at us and did not stop for a very long time. This seventeen-year-old boy was no longer in his world but one that was totally strange and seemingly very dangerous if I didn't do as told. There was an adrenalin rush of fear that went through me as I ran toward the bus door. For the next seven days, we were getting haircuts, vaccines, clothing, and miscellaneous things.

Then on April 21, 1964 I was assigned to E Company, Ninth Battalion, Third Training Brigade, or short term E-9-3. The guys I came from Detroit with were put into the same platoon I was. When we got to the training area, it was more yelling, running, and pushups. I was put in the Fifth Platoon, along with fifty-one other guys. We would be together for the next month, and at the end we knew without a doubt that our butts belonged to Uncle Sam.

We learned quickly to look out for one another because if one screwed up, the whole squad or platoon would be punished. There is a reason for that, and the sooner we learned it, the easier our lives would become. When guys got on each other's nerves, they took it into a room, getting it straightened out between them.

I remember Rasmussen, who was in charge from Detroit, and a guy from West Virginia went into the room. They stayed in there for about fifteen minutes, with everything being turned over and destroyed. When they came out, they still did not like each other, but they respected each other and that was what was needed.

We had what they called a fire watch at night, and everyone took their turn staying up for the two-hour watch. It was a stupid thing to have, but that was the army for you. We were very fortunate because we had Sgt. Martin as our platoon sergeant. He was a Korean War veteran with a combat infantryman badge and was one of the best DI's in the company. There was also a sergeant first class from the next platoon who was a mean, drunken bully. He came in our barracks one night as drunk as a skunk, slapping around some guys then yelling for us to get out in the street, pretty much making our existence a nightmare. Sgt. Martin was two stripes below him, but he raised the roof with the first sergeant about it, and the sergeant first class was gone the next day.

The best day in basic training was when we were issued our weapons and started going to the rifle range. Some of those boys from the hills could sure shoot. About halfway through basic, someone a couple of barracks over got a Dear John letter. He took it very hard, and the next thing we heard was a rifle shot. He stole a round from the rifle range, ending his life over some girl back home. This would be called a permanent solution to a temporary problem. I would find out what it was like to want to end my life later when alcoholism and PTSD took over my soul.

I learned that even though my life had been a pain up to this point, there were guys who had gone through much worse than I had. I did not like the way some of the guys were treated because of race, not only by the locals but also by some of the military personnel. At the end of basic, my platoon took honors in the battalion when it came to close order drill. It meant a great deal to us at the time because we had worked hard to get there. It amazed me how many family members came to the graduation and no I had none from my family present. Most of them were local, within a three-state region, which is probably why so many showed up. After graduating from basic training on May 21, 1964, I was given a leave with orders to report to Ft. Gordon, Georgia, on July 3.

I went back to Freeland, Michigan, which was a waste of time because it was the same people doing the same things. Why would I have thought anything would change? It had only been a few months since I left. Five years later when I went back, it would still be the same people doing the same things.

I took a bus down to Georgia, and it had to be the longest ride I ever had. I saw some beautiful country but also met some really strange people. There was a guy who pulled a knife and stuck it into my side while I was on the bus over two dollars. I didn't figure my life was worth two dollars so I gave him the money. Besides, at the time I didn't have a clue how to defend myself against a knife. Just because you graduate from basic doesn't mean you're a killing machine.

Upon arriving at Ft. Gordon, Georgia, I was assigned to an eight-week lineman course. At this school we learned to climb telephone poles and string communication wire in both combat and peacetime situations. I would be doing this in some form or another for the next forty-three years, but when I look back, the days of being a lineman give me the most satisfaction.

It is amazing the things you can do even though you are scared out of your wits—for example, the process of learning to climb telephone poles with only a small piece of steel (gaff) sticking into the pole holding you up. Most of us spent more time falling off the poles the first couple days than we did climbing. The first time I made it all the way to the top of the pole was like I had conquered the world. Didn't know it at the time, but my first cousin Gus Delucia had gone through this same course as his secondary MOS for Special Forces.

One guy came off the pole, putting a piece of wood through his bicep muscle, and then when he hit the ground, his gaff went through the top of his foot. He pulled the wood out and went back up the pole. Climbing poles was one of the greatest enjoyments I ever experienced. The highest I climbed on wood was a 75-foot wooden pole in Korea. Then there was a 106-foot tower in Vitry le François, France that we would race to the top to see who would buy the next round of beer. It was a twelve-inch triangle, so you had to be careful on that one. That's why most of the time we did it drunk.

I had a great time in Ft. Gordon, making some good friends I would serve with for the next fifteen months. We had an incident one weekend where it seemed like the whole barracks went nuts from booze and fighting. I got smacked a few times, but after they realized I could take a punch without going down, they left me alone. It started with about five guys coming back from town drunk and another guy said something to one of them. If we would have been smart, the rest of us would have thrown all five of them off the second-floor balcony. One guy was really messed up during roll call on Monday morning, but he never said who he got into it with. I heard later that the guy who messed him up went to Ft. Leavenworth, Kansas, for killing someone.

Four of us went to town one weekend to get a tattoo of a naked woman climbing a telephone pole. This thing was huge because it went from your shoulder down to your elbow. Luckily we stopped at a bar before we got to the tattoo parlor, and three of us decided to stay and drink instead of getting the tattoo. The next morning the other guy showed us his brand-new tattoo, and what a monster. I have often wondered over the years how he explained it to his children and grandchildren. I was not old enough to drink in public places, but we would sit in booths with the guys buying extra. Most of the bars looked the other way back then, which they don't do today.

Chapter 9

Just before graduation, everyone was wondering where they would be stationed, with most of us going to Korea. I had never heard of it, only to find out later that my Dad spent time there before coming back to the states after WWII. There was Bill Slobodnik, Ron White, Jesse Yowell, Tom Zahare, Ray Hopkins, and myself, with everyone except Hopkins going to Company C, 127th Signal Battalion of the Seventh Infantry Division. This was on September 9, 1964, and we would be there for the next thirteen months.

Korea at that time was the best-kept secret in the army, and for a seventeen-year-old private, it was an eye opener. We left Ft. Gordon, going directly to Korea. The first thing I experienced when I got to Kimpo Airport outside of Seoul was the smell. I don't know if they still do it, but at that time, they used human waste to fertilize their rice paddies and the smell was overpowering. By the time I left there, it was just another smell.

I was stationed at Camp Casey just south of the demilitarized zone (DMZ). I was assigned to the wire platoon for eight months until I was picked to be the captain's driver. When I walked into the wire platoon barracks on the first night, everyone wanted to know where I was from in the States and if I liked to drink. The sergeants in the platoon turned me on to Old Crow and Southern Comfort when I first got there. There was an enlisted men's club on post where you could run up a bar tab to a certain amount depending on your rank. The house boys who were hired to do our laundry and keep the barracks clean would also lend out money for interest. I always had payments to both at the end of every month due to my alcohol consumption. The wire platoon was by far the best duty I had. For a first-duty station, I could not have asked for a better one.

Across the road from the main gate was the village of Tong Du Chon, and I spent every spare minute I had there. At the time it was what we called a village of about a thousand people. You could get anything you wanted there—booze, prostitutes, and drugs. I never got into drugs while I was in the army, but I sure sampled the booze and prostitutes as much as I could.

It was a dirty place with little drainage ditches running alongside what they called a street but what we would call an alley. Then there were smaller alleys running off from the main one. It was incredibly easy in the beginning to get lost in it, but there was always some prostitute who was willing to take you back to the main gate for a fee. It had an open market, with the meat and produce hanging out in the elements. When you were going back to the post at night, it was nothing to see rats chewing on the meat and produce. This would be the same food you knew someone would be eating the next night, including the rat, when they went to the village.

One of our company dogs came up missing one day, with most of the company believing one of the house boys took it home to eat. After a little time there, you never gave a thought as to what you were eating or drinking. I sat there one night and watched mama-san kill a rat and then cook it up for this sergeant who had been abusive to her. It was hilarious the next day telling him what he ate the night before and then watching him heave his guts out. He had it coming because she didn't deserve what he did to her. Most people in the rural areas of Korea liked the US military because they still remembered what had happened just ten years previously.

One night I was crossing the railroad tracks into the village, and when I looked to my right, there, half-covered by a straw mat, laid a young women with her head cut off. Her body was there for two days before they picked it up. Her American boyfriend had gone back to the States and didn't take her with him like he promised. She couldn't stand the thought of losing him, so after getting drunk, she placed her neck on the tracks as a train came through.

I learned quickly that life was cheap there. The only time the village would be off limits was when an American was killed there. I lost a good friend who was a cook in our company for a while and then went into the CID, which is an investigative branch of the military police. He and his partner both died on the same night in the village, but we never heard how, why, or what took place. Our company commander got a letter from his mother later saying he died in Vietnam. I don't know how she came up with that story.

I was promoted to the rank of SP/4 E-4 while there even though I received three article fifteens, one for being in an off-limits place, another for having alcohol in the company area, and the last for a curfew violation. The two that do not mention alcohol were caused because I was being drunk and stupid. There was also the time I came back to the company area drenched in blood. The only problem was it was mine. The guy who sucker punched me was originally from our company, and he sure could pack a punch. Just before he went back to the States, he stopped by the company area and apologized. He was stoned that night and didn't want his Korean girlfriend to know he was smoking dope—as if she didn't already know. I was drunk with him being stoned, and then people wonder why asinine things happen.

We were a tight group in Korea, with the wire platoon guys sticking together. On one miserably cold night, I had an overnight pass to stay in the village but no place to stay and no money for a room because I had drank it up. I figured that was not a problem; I would go and sleep on the porch of a buddy's hooch. I must have passed out because the next thing I remember is Jeff and his girl dragging me into the hooch during the middle of the night. I probably would have frozen to death if not for what they did. How the Korean veterans fought a war there is beyond me.

We had a building where the company toilets, showers, and sinks were located. I came back from town one winter night drunk and started to tear the place apart. I was starting to get mean when I drank, and that was not healthy for me or anyone else. This guy from another platoon started to mop the floor with my drunken behind when the guys from the wire platoon came running. That ended the butt kicking even though I had it coming. I stopped caring about how anyone felt. I was going to do what I wanted to do. If that meant getting punched out then that was part of the price you paid. I was close to the men in my platoon, and whatever took place elsewhere was too bad.

They had specific bars for the different units in the village, and if you went into the wrong one, you got hurt very quickly. One night after a couple of hours of drinking, I wandered into an infantry bar. They let me get to the center of the bar before they came at me. I think I got one or two swings in before I went down. As I lay there on the floor being punched and kicked, I could feel guys being yanked off me. Three Turkish soldiers had come in and decided to help this dumb, drunken American signalman out of the mess he had gotten himself into. The fight didn't last long once they pulled their knives. You did not mess with the Turks over there. If they caught anyone stealing, they hung them by the neck at their front gate and left them there for a while.

Another time I went to a black bar looking for Yowell. I started yelling for Jesse as soon as I went through the door, which was good because they came at me the moment they realized I was in their bar. If it hadn't been for Jesse getting me out of there as quickly as he did, I would probably have gotten stabbed or killed that night. The stupidity of a drunk can never be understated.

One of our trucks broke down in what was called Smuggler's Gap on the way to a field exercise in the middle of the night. I never saw the guys in the truck until we got back to the company area, where we were told they had been taken by a North Korean patrol that was using the gap to try to get back to the North. A South Korean patrol intercepted them on the way to the border, releasing our guys.

Another time an officer had three of us draw weapons and ammo, and we went looking for some Koreans who he had been involved with, later finding out they were North Korean infiltrators. We never did find them, and I can't remember exactly what it was all about. My first cousin Sfc. Auggie Delucia was involved with intercept missions in early 1968 as part of a Special Forces A-team on the DMZ. He told me later they terminated a few North Korean teams coming into South Korea before his team went back to Okinawa.

There was another instance when the mayor of Ui Jong Bu and his entire family were assassinated by a squad of North Koreans. I had been arrested earlier that night for drunk and disorderly conduct and was waiting for the company to come and get me out of jail. It could be a dangerous place around the DMZ in the early sixties, but in the mid-sixties it really heated up. The captain and I went to the DMZ one day to check communications. We spent the night there, and it was an adrenaline rush looking across no man's land. It was a whole different world from Camp Casey even though we were only a few miles apart. I liked the rough and tumble world that was Korea during that time.

I never went any farther south than Seoul, which I was glad of because it was too much like the States. One winter night we were on patrol, and I remember going over this small hill into a village. It was about one o'clock in the morning and bone-chilling cold. There was a full moon, and the ground was covered with about a foot and a half of snow. The squad leader stopped us and went to a hut, returning a few moments later with a bottle of Korean whiskey. As I stood there in the moonlight, the sergeant took a drink and then passed the bottle around. When it got to me, I took a couple of big swallows and still remember the warmth spreading as it started at the top of my head and slowly went to the bottom of my feet. I could not believe how good that warmth felt or how relaxed it made me.

On the last night I spent in Korea, I went to the village even though the replacement center said we weren't allowed to go there. There was beer to be consumed, and besides, I wanted to see this certain bar girl one last time. Who were they to tell this eighteen-year-old veteran of Korea anything? I had come to Korea as a bewildered seventeen-year-old kid and left thirteen months later screwed up. I had no idea I was on my way to insanity.

My next assignment was Ft. Huachuca, Arizona, and I only spent thirty days there. I went to the 459th Signal Battalion, and who should I see there at my first formation but most of the guys I was in Korea with. After talking with them a little while, I knew this was not for me. There was no way I could survive the army within the continental United States. I would not be able to handle the crap that was dished out Stateside—not to mention I didn't like all the sand, snakes, and scorpions Arizona had.

On October 27, 1965, I re-enlisted for four more years with my duty station being Verdun, France. They gave me a reenlistment bonus of about one thousand dollars, and it would get me out of the States, so why not? I had just come off a thirty-day leave after thirteen months in Korea, and now I was getting thirty more days before I left for France because I would not be able to come back to the States unless I took leave and paid for it. Europe was a four-year assignment.

Chapter 10

Butch married Sue Simmerman from Midland, Michigan, while I was in Korea. She was the only woman I ever saw who could shut him up when he was in one of his drunken rants. Their first child was named Jeff, he was barely a month old when I came back from Korea, and now thirty days later I was coming back to get her husband drunk every night for thirty more days. She was one of the kindest women I ever met. I don't ever recall a time when she raised her voice toward anyone, but that didn't interfere with the steel resolve that coursed through her veins. She was a strong woman who had certain values she lived by.

There was an incident before Butch quit drinking when he came home after the bars closed and got her out of bed while telling her to cook him eggs. He told me later she never said a word but made the eggs extra runny and hash browns with bacon, and when they were done, she poured them over his head and went back to bed. That was the kind of woman she was, and I believe he was very fortunate to have her as his wife and the mother of his children. Sue was a very devoted Christian, and later in their marriage, Butch became one also. She gave freely of herself in both time and money, and she loved her family deeply.

Sue had two younger sisters, one of whom I was involved with when I was on leave this time. By involved I mean we saw each other once in a while and drank together at Butch's. The other one I later married when the military was behind me. My main source of pleasure in life was women and drinking. It didn't matter in what order, but later in my drinking career it would be booze first. I would like to say I was a happy drunk, but that was not the case. I could get mean at the least provocation, and the blackouts had already started. I was turning into what I thought I would never be and didn't even know it.

The old man and Barb were married and had a son named Joe. They would have a daughter later named Chris. I spent a fairly uneventful thirty days at home, with Butch and me drinking up my reenlistment bonus. It was thirty days before we had drank up all the money I had saved while in Korea. I think Sue was glad to see me leave for Europe, and the thought of not seeing me for four years probably sounded very good to her. I was even glad when it was over and I could go back.

Chapter 11

I left out of Ft. Dix, New Jersey, arriving at Orly International Airport in Paris, France. I then took a train up to the Maginot Caserne, Verdun, France, reporting in at the 256th Signal Company (SVC). The train ride was interesting because I didn't have a room of my own but had to stand in the hallway of the railroad car the whole way. It was like in the movies, with the hallway on one side of the train car and glass windows all along the side. I saw a lot of beautiful country while sipping French beer.

I stayed at Verdun until December 30, 1965, when I reported to Detachment B, 532nd Signal Company. This was an army medical depot, and we supplied microwave and HF frequency radio capabilities plus a local dial tone. The only bad part of my reenlistment was that I was no longer a lineman. I found I hated dial tone, probably because I had never been properly trained in it.

This was at Vitry Le Francois, France, and the major thing I learned there was not to gamble. One payday after receiving my money, I went to the enlisted men's club, started drinking, and lost my whole month's wages playing slot machines in about five hours. That is a drunk's worst nightmare, and after that I never put more than a couple of bucks into a slot machine. There was an older French woman who owned a bar-restaurant a few kilometers outside of town in this small village. I learned she was involved with the French underground during WWII and was highly decorated by both the United States and France. She always treated us well when we went there. There were pictures of her when she was younger on the wall, and she was very pretty.

I got into a lot of trouble because of my drinking while I was attached to this unit. They had a Depot Day Celebration with steaks, booze, and games for the children of the dependents. For some reason, I started drinking hard stuff early, not lasting too much past mid-afternoon. I was on my knees eating a steak off the ground when Moose, a mountain of a man who happened to be a medic, put me up over his shoulder and carried me back to the barracks, dropping me on my bunk.

Some of us were in town drinking one night, and I tried to dive out of a second-story window. This would not have been noteworthy, but it was in an apartment of one of the married guys from the detachment. He and his wife were not used to that sort of behavior and acted accordingly, turning me into the detachment commander. We had been doing it back at base, but it was always feet first. Because I was drunk, I wanted to go head first. The detachment commander didn't think it was a good idea either, putting alcohol off limits for me for the next thirty days. It was a long thirty days, but I didn't learn what I should have because it was not the last time I got into trouble because of booze.

I had some friends in the medics, and there were a couple of cooks who could get what we needed to make our own brew. That was some wicked stuff and would take the back of your head off. On May 11, 1966, I made sergeant and celebrated by getting hammered. I lived in a two-man room with Sgt. Lavalle from Massachusetts, and I have to say he was way crazier than I ever thought of being. Every time we got drunk, we would end up fighting one another. During one fight we got into, he tried to burn my eyes out with a lit cigarette. When he finally accepted the fact I wasn't going to let him do that, he quit trying. Both of us were pretty bruised up after that one.

Alcohol makes you do dumb things. Even with all the fighting we did with each other, I would say we got along fairly well. If you walked out of our room and turned left, you walked into the enlisted men's club. Coming back from the club one day, we got into a fight, and our beds and a few other things went out the window. The sergeant major of the medical depot caught us and chewed us out until we had nothing left to chew on; then he made us carry everything back up to the room. Oh yeah, guess who talked me into jumping out of second-floor windows?

We also had a big guy from the Louisiana swamps we nicknamed Frenchy because he spoke Cajun French in the unit. He loved to drink and fight and enjoyed life to the fullest. He became best friends with a little guy from Pennsylvania who happened to be a Mennonite. After the Cajun took this Mennonite under his wing, he couldn't get enough booze in him and thought he could whip the world. They looked like Mutt and Jeff going down the road, and a lot of the time the Cajun would have the little guy slung over his shoulder, carrying him back from wherever they got drunk.

I was assigned to Detachment A, 532nd Signal Company on March 17, 1966. This unit was located at

Nancy, France, which is a very beautiful area of France. I was a cable splicer while I was there, which was another thing I had never been trained in. Have you ever tried to solder something with a blowtorch?

While I was there I met Christine, a military dependent. She was fifteen, I was nineteen, and we became very close because she was having a rough time at home. We met on a bus that carried us guys into town and at the same time picked up military dependents, bringing them to the post. We never became intimate, which was good because the legal age of consent in the military was sixteen. We stayed friends for as long as I was there and then again when I came back on temporary duty (TDY). One of her friends was seeing a buddy of mine, and I later heard they got married. Christine's dad didn't want her hanging out with anyone in the military so we would meet downtown and go for walks in the woods or to a movie. She was very special to me.

While in France I acquired a taste for cognac and coke, which I would chase with a Heineken. It wasn't the Heineken that you get in the States. This was a lot stronger and much better tasting. I met Pfc. George Gibbs while I was at Nancy, and we followed each other from unit to unit until I left Europe. He showed me how to use a knife and also how to protect myself from a straight razor. He drew a forty-five-caliber pistol on me when I tried to get inside a restricted area in which he worked when I was drunk. He warned me several times not to come through the door or he would shoot. If I hadn't stopped, he would have shot me because those were the standing orders for that room. That was another instance when drinking almost got me killed.

I don't remember who the guy was, but he went to Nancy one night, getting in a fight with a Frenchman. The Frenchman used a cane sword on him, but he didn't think it was serious, so he came back to the barracks and went to bed. We found him in the morning unconscious, lying in a pool of blood. They got him to the hospital and saved his life, but he never came back to the unit. I don't know if they caught the guy who stuck him.

On May 9, 1966, I was sent to Orleans, France, to take part in the First Signal Group Organization Day activities. I can't recall what took place down there, but I remember sitting at an outside cafe looking toward a statue of Joan of Arc on a horse (Joannie on the pony). I remember it was an impressive work of art and extremely big.

In June of 1966 Carol married Don Manary from Midland, and they moved to Jacksonville, Florida, where he was stationed in the navy, so I never met him until I came back from Europe. I didn't find out until forty some years later that he was in naval intelligence with a rating so high I had never heard of it. He still can't talk about what he did there.

He didn't take anything from Grandma Spencer or anyone else in the family. When he and Carol got married, they became one, and that was the way he lived it. I had words with Carol through the mail once and he told me to screw off, so that was enough to make me like the guy. I can't ever remember being mad at him, even during my worst drinking days. I knew he didn't always like what I did, but I was his wife's brother and that was that. Later in life Don went through bypass surgery and cancer, but I never heard him complain about any of it. He took it all in stride and lives his life on a moment-by-moment basis.

Like Sue, his family is his whole life. They had two children, a son named Dennis and a daughter named Stacie. I could not have asked for better spouses for my sister or brother. Don couldn't help it if he was in the navy.

On June 30, 1966, I was again assigned to Detachment B, 532nd Signal Company being put on temporary duty back at Nancy, France. During this time Christine's dad was reassigned to a unit in Germany. It was a sad day when it was time for her to leave because we had become very close so maybe there was still a soft spot in me somewhere. Later when I was in Germany, I received a call from her telling me she had been seeing a psychologist and my name had been brought up. She didn't know if I would get in trouble, but she wanted to let me know. She said she was going back to live with her aunt in the States because she couldn't take it at home anymore. About a year after I was out of the military, I was watching *The Newlywed Game* when who should I see but Christine and her husband. They looked very happy together. I wish her well wherever she is and hope she's had a good life.

A short time later I was assigned back to the 256th Signal Company in Verdun. On September 26, 1966, they sent SP/4 John Nasello and me to Orleans for ten days to do cable mapping. John wanted to take his personal car and that was approved, so we had transportation while there. This was a large hospital complex where all the telephone cables ran in a two-and-a-half-foot crawl space under the buildings. The thing they forgot to tell us was the crawl space was also home to feral cats. I thought we were going to have a heart attack the first time we ran into them, but we started carrying pistols, and that was the end to a bunch of cats. We also uncovered an unexploded bazooka round while we were under there. It must have been left over from WWII and was never found when they were building the complex. The ordnance guys recovered it and blew it up in a field.

On the weekend we were off duty, and Nasello wanted to go see Paris, so off we went. We got there late in the afternoon and started sightseeing. We started out at the Arc De Triomphe and moved around from there. We drank constantly while sightseeing, so by the end of the night we were pretty well blitzed. The one place both of us wanted to go was called Pig Alley. This was a street, and at the end of it was the Moulin Rouge Theater. All the windows on the street had women in them showing their wares and inviting you in to sample. Remember, this was back in 1966, and to a young guy from the Midwest this was a genuine smorgasbord.

The next morning I woke up in the backseat of Nesello's car, and we were parked on a side street next to the Eiffel Tower. It felt like I had been hit in the head with a baseball bat and somebody had poured sand in my mouth. I didn't know where I was at first—just that a man and a woman were looking into the car window at us. One of the doors was open, and there were beer bottles scattered everywhere. I woke up Nasello, and we got out of there before the gendarmes came, giving us a longer stay in Paris.

We went back to Verdun shortly after our trip to Paris. There was a great deal of history at Verdun and the surrounding area. Looking back I wish I had seen more, but that was not on my priority list at the time. There was a bar where the French Army and the French Foreign Legion hung out when they rotated between

France and Algeria. I met a bunch of crazy guys there, but the one I still remember was Jean Claude, who also attracted every woman who came into the place. Women would actually fight over who was going to sit next to him. I don't remember him taking it seriously even though he was never alone when he left the bar. He was just an all-around great guy to hang out with, and you also had your pick of what was left.

Verdun was where I had my first taste of white lightning. There were some guys from the hills of Kentucky, and they would get care packages of the stuff in the mail. After mail call one day, a buddy offered me some he had just received. I remember taking about three swallows and then instantly blacking out. It was like that every time I drank it.

A guy in our platoon received notification that his mother had died. He was supposed to leave the next day to go home, but that night he started drinking. By nine o'clock he was sitting outside on the third-floor ledge, drinking, crying, and saying he was going to jump. I think every one of us went on that ledge to talk him back in. I don't remember who finally talked him in, but he did eventually come in.

On November 29, 1966, the company received orders to move to Germany because President Charles De Gaulle was kicking all American military forces out of France. After everything we had done for France during WWI and WWII it came down to that. I lost a very close friend during this move when a truck he was driving loaded with bombs went over a cliff. His name was Ernie Castro, and he was an only child. It still irritates me when I think of the unfairness of his death. He had volunteered to go to the transportation unit to drive, and it got him killed. I think of Charles De Gaulle in the same way I do Jane Fonda, and that makes them both bottom feeders.

It was sometime in November of 1966 that I went to Verdun one night to have a few beers and see what I could get into. At about ten o'clock I ran into Willie Naranjo, a Navajo Indian from New Mexico. We had been buddies for a long time, but that night I was the enemy because Sergeant Benton had told Willie earlier I had smacked him around. He was not happy about it and was planning on taking out his anger on me. And no, I had not punched the guy out, but I sure wanted to afterward. Somehow we got a French car involved in the scrap because I tore things off the car to use on Willie, who was much bigger than me. The next thing I knew the military police and French gendarmes had us both in handcuffs, and we were heading to jail. The captain wanted to get involved but couldn't because the French police were charging us.

Unknown to us at the time, our defense lawyer was the executive officer of our company, a Captain Clemenceau. I was told his great-grandfather was the prime minister of France in WWI. Willie got out of going to court because he was shipped to Germany ahead of the main company to set things up for our move. If I remember right, the charges were drunk and disorderly with destruction of private property. It cost me a little over ninety francs to pay the fine and court costs. You would think that I should have learned something from this, but sad to say, I was still caught up in being stupid.

On February 1, 1967, I spent the night in Verdun, not making it back for roll call. There was alcohol, a good-looking woman lying next to me, and a bad hangover that made it hard to get out of bed that morning. As soon as I got back I was sent to the company commander, who yelled at me, making my head hurt even worse than it did. Then he asked me what I thought he should do with my sergeant stripes. I was still drunk, telling him I didn't give a damn what he did with the stripes. That was the end of my being a sergeant in his company.

Thirty years later I sent for my military records, and he stated in them that he had been counseling me about my drinking problem. That was the first and last time I ever saw the captain so there wasn't any talk between him and me about my drinking. I don't remember anyone in the 256th Signal Company (SVC) ever mentioning my drinking, but it was definitely the drinking and my mouth that caused me to lose the stripes. When they said, "An Article 15 with loss of rank," I could not have cared less.

On March 8, 1967, seven of us with our platoon sergeant went to Bar Le Duc, France, to take down some old lead cable before we left for Germany. Our platoon sergeant was Staff Sergeant Addison R. Elsholz, a veteran of the Korean War. He had one eye that was messed up, wore the Bronze Star with V device and the Purple Heart, and was one of the finest men I have ever met. He would invite me to his room, and we would sit around drinking and talking about whatever came up.

One question I always seemed to ask him was, "When do you realize you have become a man?" He would take a drink of whiskey, smile, and tell me, "Phil, you will know when you know." Whenever I am asked who had the most impact on my life, his face is the one I see, even after all these years.

We spent six days at Bar Le Duc, France, and it was great because I was back to doing line work. Every night we went to the same café, which happened to be a college hangout, and drank until it closed. It got to the point where they would automatically bring us a case of beer when we walked in the door.

The last day we were taking down cable over a gorge with the bridge about fifteen feet from the cable. It was a couple of hundred feet to the bottom of the gorge, and none of us wanted any part of that span. The way we did it was to turn our safety belts around, and after running them through the d-rings, we hooked them to the steel strand and would sit in our belts while pulling ourselves across the span. On this span we knew the cable was going to run back at us with a big loop in the middle dragging you downward.

The guy who got picked was Dennis Weaver from West Virginia. He took it very slow, but as he got to the middle, it ran back on him like we thought, pulling him down. We tied him off with extra ropes in case the strand broke. If it did, at least we would have him and he would not fall far. When he cut the wire holding that lead cable, I've never seen anyone go for such a ride. He shot twenty feet into the air, and then for a very long time, he bounced up and down until finally coming to a stop. After we realized he was okay, all of us fell on the road laughing so hard it hurt. Weaver called us every name he could think of. We pulled him over to the pole, and when he climbed down, he let us know there would be no more climbing for him that day. It's always rough being the low man on the totem pole.

That night when we left the bar, there were ten empty beer cases sitting there as we staggered out. When we got back to the company area they were ready to move, so we saddled up and headed for Germany, arriving there in late March 1967.

Chapter 12

The French people didn't like us much unless we were in the rural areas. There was something about the French that made them think they were a little better than everyone else. I think the United States has that same character flaw now. France had been okay, but it was a dirty country compared to Germany. Even the woods in Germany were picked clean of twigs and fallen brush.

Germany was the beginning of the end for me when it came to staying in Europe. I was in the last bunch of our company to leave France, arriving at Kreuzberg Caserne Zweibrucken, Germany, on March 31, 1967. It was very picturesque where we were, with rolling hills, little villages, and the town of Zweibrucken itself. There was a river that ran through the town where you could rent paddle boats and they would let you take your beer in them. I left an expensive pair of binoculars in one of those boats while I was drunk. What we called fairs would come to town, and of course, the biggest tents were where you could buy beer and food. I didn't like most of the beer because it was too thick, but they did have some that was okay. It was stronger that the stuff I drank in France.

In the surrounding area of Zweibrucken there was the US Army, the US Air Force, and the Canadian Air

Force. Needless to say, when we came together in those beer tents, there was always trouble to be had. You knew where the fights were because there would be a roar and everyone would get on top of the picnic-style tables to watch the fight. We were sitting there one night with our backs to the Canadians when a Canadian kept shoving the guy sitting next to me. Tex was a big boy and didn't like being messed with, so during about the second shove, Tex let the Canadian have it upside his head with an elbow. The guy dropped like a rock as his buddies came over the table for us. I believe the cops came to stop this one because it got out of hand with the whole tent going nuts.

Just before I left the company, Tex was drunk and for some reason decided to take me apart. As he jumped over a second-floor stairwell to get me, I bolted for the door because Tex was not a guy you wanted pissed at you. I made it out the door, but Tex was so drunk he couldn't keep up so I got away. I asked him later what brought all of that about, and he didn't know. He just wanted to fight!

I bought a 9 mm Walters P-38 while there at the local sportsmen club. It had the original holster with two clips. Another guy and I took it to the firing range to see how it would do. After putting four clips through it, one of the rounds came zinging past my left ear. I didn't know it at the time, but that would not be the last time I would hear rounds going by my ears. This was the same club where one of the guys from our company who had never drunk before decided he wanted to try it. We watched him down one pitcher, and when he started the second, he brought it up drinking the whole thing. As he lowered the pitcher he filled it up with puke and then drank that back down.

We carried him out of there after that. I believe that little excursion cured him of drinking again while I was there.

I was at the enlisted men's club at closing time, and for some reason, I wanted to punch out this German civilian, but as I went for him, his buddies got in the way, and the next thing I knew there was a riot going on. Once again the military police were called to break it up. The bouncers that night were friends of mine, with one of them being Gibbs. He ripped me a new one the next morning, telling me in no uncertain terms that I had been in the wrong and was on everyone's list. Thank you, Mr. John Barleycorn!

During this time, SSgt. Elsholz took me under his wing, for he could see where I was headed, and tried to intervene. It was also during this period of my drinking career that I started pissing my pants or would get diarrhea when drunk. I was also wetting the bed because I was too drunk to wake up. This wasn't every time but often enough. There is nothing worse than walking back from town after you had the runs or pissed your pants. Needless to say I was a mess and just kept getting messier, no pun intended. I was losing any friends I might have had and was wearing out my welcome at the 256th Signal Company (SVC).

On July 13, 1967, we were re-designated as the USASTRATCOMEUR Signal Service Unit. That didn't mean anything to me because I was looking for a way to get out of there and didn't care where I went. I talked with SSgt. Elsholz, and he suggested I talk to the first sergeant. After I met with him, it was decided that a little country in Asia would be a good match for me. The first sergeant didn't care as long as I left his company. That sounded good to me, and I put in a transfer, not caring what type of unit I went to as long as I went somewhere. I wish I had given it more thought. I would have put in for an infantry division again instead of where they assigned me. SSgt. Elsholz thought it was a good idea but warned me to keep my head down and not to volunteer for anything. I believe he thought some combat would straighten me out.

On October 7, 1967, orders came down for me to report to USARV Transient Detachment in the republic of South Vietnam no later than December 1, 1967, with ultimate assignment to First Signal Brigade. I left Rein Main Air Force Base in Frankfurt, Germany, reporting to Fort Hamilton, Brooklyn, New York, on October 17, 1967. I was to be on leave, reporting to the overseas replacement station in Oakland, California at no later than 1200 hours on November 29, 1967. It sounds ridiculous that someone would leave the relative safety of Europe to go to a combat zone, but it made perfect sense to me at the time and still makes sense today. It's called a geographical change, and I would make more of them later in life.

Chapter 13

My sister-in-law was going to be bothered by her husband's drunken brother once again. How she put up with me coming back on leave all the time I will never know. I don't remember much of what happened during this leave because I had lots of money to drink on and who knew if I would make it back, so let's drink and be stupid. Sue's youngest sister, Peggy, would watch Jeff, their baby, when we did go out. I always bought a Texas Fifth when I came back, and it would be gone when I left. I'm not sure how many fifths it held, but it was a few. I wasn't twenty-one yet so did most of my drinking at people's homes.

Mom had married a man named Duane LaFreinere, and they were living in a trailer court on Dixie Road in Saginaw at the time. I liked Duane; he was a straight shooter and was always sincere in how he treated people. I went to their place about once a week, getting drunk every time and then driving back to Freeland. If I got pulled over by the police, they would take me home rather than to jail. It was like that back then because the laws were not strict when it came to drunk driving. If they had given me a ticket for all the times I was pulled over, I could have papered the walls of an outhouse. The insanity of getting into a vehicle and driving after you've been drinking makes no sense, but that is what drunks do. If you don't think so all you have to do is read the papers.

I received a call from my first love while I was on leave this time. I still remember her walking into the first grade, and I thought she was the prettiest girl I had ever seen. When it was time for recess, I went directly to her, planting a kiss on her cheek. I want to tell you that didn't go over well with her or the teacher. Thank God it wasn't like it is today. I would have probably been locked up for sexual assault. Needless to say, I stayed away from Tammy Jo Hanley after that. There was and always will be a tender spot in my heart for Tammy even though we didn't hang out together growing up.

We saw each other on and off for the week she was visiting. I stopped at Chicago, where she lived, on my way to Vietnam, drinking up what little booze she and her roommates had in their apartment. When I set down on her couch, she climbed into my lap, staying there until it was time for me to leave. It surprised me but at the same time felt natural for her to be there. We talked to each other softly so no one else could hear us. We were face-to-face with the smell of her surrounding me and those deep, penetrating eyes she had looking right through to my soul. To this day I don't know why she did it, but I'm glad she did.

Tammy was a stewardess for United Airlines at the time. I found out later she made flights to Vietnam delivering fresh meat and then bringing the guys who had finished their tours back to the States. I glanced back toward her apartment while I was waiting for the taxi, and she was standing in the window watching. She stayed there until the taxi came, and it dawned on me that this might very well be the last time I would ever see her. I wanted to go back in and be with her longer, but there was no time left. The thought was fleeting, but it moved me as I contemplated that it would be sad to never see her again.

On November 30, 1967, I was at the army personnel center in Oakland, California, and they had assigned me to the First Signal Brigade USASTRATCOM in the republic of South Vietnam. If I thought the flight to Korea or Europe had been long, the one to Vietnam seemed like an eternity. We landed in the afternoon at Bien Hoa Air Base, and when I got to the plane's door, the heat and smell were overwhelming. It was like stepping into an oven with the smell being the next attention grabber. As I took a deep breath, I knew I was home at last. Unknown to me, I had left part of myself in Korea, and now I had found that piece in Vietnam. It was like I was finally home, and it felt good. It's hard to explain, but there are those out there who know exactly what I mean.

They took us to the Ninetieth Replacement Battalion at Long Bien Post. The bus had mesh wire over the windows in case someone wanted to give us a hand grenade welcoming present on the way to Long Bien. It was there a two-foot lizard used me as a landing pad when he came out of a tree with the VC dropping mortars on us at night. I made a mental decision while I was at the Ninetieth to accept what was ahead of me even though I didn't know what it would be. There was some fear, apprehension, and more adrenalin flowing in me than normal. We were definitely not in Kansas anymore, and Toto was nowhere to be found.

Chapter 14

On December 4, 1967, they assigned me to the 160th Signal Group, and on December 8, I was assigned to Co. A, Fortieth Signal Battalion, which was where I would spend the next year and a half. The company area was on Long Bien Post, and I was assigned to the Second Platoon.

I want to say I was not in the infantry while I was in Vietnam. I had close friends who were, and they went through some of the worst combat that was fought over there. I had a buddy who transferred to the infantry, coming back a few months later to visit with the Combat Infantrymen's Badge on his chest. He wanted me and a few of the other old-timers to transfer to his unit. He said we could have a ball while getting back together. I have often wondered if he made it home in one piece. The men who served in the infantry, combat engineers, and artillery units deserve all the admiration and distinction that can be given them. They carried the lion's share of the load when it came to combat and should be recognized for that. I would get into it once in a while but nothing like they did. I believe I walk in the company of heroes when I am among them. Believe me when I say I don't use that word lightly.

After I settled in, I looked over into this other hooch, and there sat Ray Hopkins from AIT and Korea. He had a few days left in country, stating he came over with the company from the States. We spent the next few hours catching up as he let me know what to expect. Hopkins said Ron White, who was with us in AIT and Korea, had just left for the States. He said White kept clear of the whores in Vietnam just as he had in Korea. White was a man who loved his wife, and that was it. He said the Second Platoon was filled with a bunch of crazies and I should fit in very well.

Our platoon sergeant was a black staff sergeant who was a younger version of SSgt. Elsholz. I found out later the first thing he did when he got in country was buy a whorehouse in Saigon. His driver took him there once a month to pick up the profits. Bishop, his driver, was from Orlando, Florida, and kept us informed as to what was coming down the pike. He was a good guy to hang out with because he would try anything once.

I was finally in a construction battalion, which meant I was back in the line crews. The only thing that would have made it better was if it had been an infantry division signal unit because that was what I started out in. The platoon sergeant was not only an outstanding soldier but also a great teacher. I learned things from him that I would use for the rest of my working career. He was our platoon sergeant for most of my first year in 'Nam. Our company sent platoons all over South Vietnam from Long Bien Post, which was close to Bien Hoa on down to Ca Mau close to the South China Sea. The other companies of the battalion were spread north up to the DMZ, with some working with the Marines up there.

I spent most of my first tour in the Mekong Delta but also was in Saigon during TET 68. The Mekong Delta was mostly rice paddies, producing most of what Vietnam ate. The area up north would have been more like Korea because that was where the mountains and jungles were, and the Korea I knew was all mountains. Once I was put into the flow of things, I seldom got back to the company area. I spent Christmas and all of January at Long Bien, with the post being hit by mortars and VC probing the perimeter. I was put on the platoon digger truck with one of the older guys nicknamed Kip from Ohio. When I refer to older guys, I mean guys who had more time in country.

On the night of January 31, 1968, the crap hit the fan all over South Vietnam. It was what has become known as TET 68, with the VC exacting as much damage as they could at every place they could. We were alerted to get ready to head for Saigon at first light to start restoring communications that had been blown up. The adrenaline was pumping as we got ready, only to be told by the platoon sergeant that Kip and I would not be going. We were going with some Korean military that had came from God only knows where at first light. It really infuriated us, and we did everything we could to talk them into letting us go to Saigon with the platoon. The first sergeant finally said after we finished with the Koreans we could catch up with the platoon in the Cholon area of Saigon.

There were three Koreans in the jeep with a mounted M-60 machine gun, so we drew our supply of ammo and c-rations and followed the jeep out the front gate, not knowing where we were heading. We went through the same province I found out later the VC used to infiltrate through into Saigon. How we made it to the Korean compound without getting hit is beyond me because the VC was still pouring troops through the area that morning.

When we got to their compound, they settled us into a tent, and we got to work because we wanted to get back to the platoon. That night we were hit hard, taking some casualties. As far as Kip and I knew, we were the only Americans in this compound, so it was a fascinating time. The next day we were doing our thing, and I tripped over something. As Kip and I started to laugh about it, so did this Korean private. His corporal did not think that was appropriate, so he slapped him upside the head and started to scream at him. The unfortunate fellow must have been hit three or four times before the corporal backed off.

I can still see the embarrassment and awkwardness on the private's face. I felt sorry for the guy, but that's the way it was in the Korean army and probably still is. They were rough, and whenever I was with them, there was never a dull moment. We had a few beers with them at night, but there was no heavy drinking because we pretty much knew we would be hit every night. They had a pet snake they kept caged, feeding it live chickens when it got hungry. It had to be at least eighteen feet long and was as big around as my thigh. Later at Can Tho we kept one about the same size under a boardwalk that we placed our communication wire in. That was until another unit came in during the night, and as they started to run wire, they came upon our snake, beating it to death with a board. It's a good thing PETA wasn't around or we would have had all sorts of problems. I believe we spent no more than three days with the Koreans before we left to go find our platoon. It was a relief to get out of there because we wanted to get back with the guys.

As we made our way into Saigon, all sorts of trucks were hauling bodies outside the city to be buried or burned. There were still bodies lying where they had fallen, some VC and others civilians. Parts of the city were hit hard with heavy fighting. We found the platoon restoring communications in the Cholon area. They told us they had been taking fire on and off since they got there. One guy said he went over the top of his truck with another guy going under when some grenades came their way. We were told to go out to the side as flankers, and shortly afterward the guy next to me yelled to look back and up. There was a Vietnamese prop plane coming in, and he had just released one of his bombs. It sailed just over our heads. What an adrenalin rush the first time you see something like that.

It took some time for the VC to be killed or captured and even longer for us to get communications back to where they were before the attacks. The national press and television stations in the States were reporting that we were getting overrun throughout the country and the VC were hammering us. Thank you for not only turning the public against the war but also against the men and women who were fighting it. They can say what they want, but I know from being there that the VC were wiped out as an effective fighting force during these attacks. The national press and television didn't report the news; they manipulated it. They had an agenda they wanted to put forth, and they did whatever it took to do that. What's troubling is forty some years later, they are still doing it.

We spent the nights on the Tan Son Nut Air Base with the Sixty-Ninth Signal Battalion. The old timers told us we could get beer at the enlisted men's club, so that sounded okay. During TET, though, you could only get a couple of beers and no more. The last thing they needed was some damn drunk out there with a weapon shooting up the place. When TET had quieted down, we did go to that club as often as we could. It wouldn't have made any difference because Saigon had bars and whorehouses all over the place. The air force had this bunker made of c-ration cases, and when we left the bunker had caved in as we ate our way through it.

After TET we were building a new pole line on one of the main streets in Saigon when out of nowhere a bunch of vehicles with gun jeeps and sirens blaring came down the street. In the middle of the convoy was Nguyen Cao Ky, who was vice president of South Vietnam at the time. I remember him looking out the window of his car and nodding at us as he went by. We were still staying with the Sixty-Ninth Signal Battalion at night, so beer was always available.

After everything was cleaned up from TET, duty in Saigon was good. There was everything a drunken soldier could want in this town. They had what was called massage parlors where you could get booze, prostitutes, massages, and saunas. They would even order you something to eat if you wanted it. There was no telling what kind of meat it would be though. The doors to the sauna opened into the heated area rather than being pushed out as you would expect. One of the guys got so drunk he fired up the sauna to the point where he couldn't breathe. The next thing we heard was him hitting the door with his shoulder, trying to get out of there. The more he hit the door, the tighter it got, finally a couple of us kicked the door in to get him out.

SP/4 Bob Bixler from Ohio and I went to get some equipment at the company area, but as we were heading out of Saigon, we got caught in a traffic jam. The white mice (Vietnamese police) were trying to straighten it out, but not much good was coming from it. Finally Bob had enough and started to go around everyone because you never knew who would drop a grenade into your lap on the way by. One of the cops pointed his weapon at us so Bob stopped the two-and-a-half-ton truck, waving the cop over. When he got to the truck, Bob motioned for him to climb up and then pointed at his lap. The dummy crawled up on the running board, but when he looked down, he turned as white as his uniform. Bob was grinning at him with his finger on the trigger of an M-3 grease gun. The cop got the message and waved us through. Bix was always fun to be around. We came in country at about the same time, so we spent a lot of time together.

Sometime around late April we headed back to the company area before going to the Delta. I ran into Sergeant Joe Hawks, who I was in Korea with, and he had been assigned to the Second Platoon. It was getting to be more like home all the time. Needless to say, we headed over to the club to catch up on what had been going on. I had not seen him since I left Ft. Huachuca, Arizona. Sergeant Hawks was the type of guy who always wanted to see how far he could push before he got shut down. One time in the Mekong Delta, Sergeant Hawks and I were drunk, eventually taking a jeep for a joy ride around town and then out into the country. Thank God we sobered up enough to realize this was not something we should be doing by ourselves, and we got our sorry behinds back to the air field. It amazes me how quickly alcohol strips you of all common sense and you do the stupidest things imaginable.

In May of 1968, Lieutenant Dennis L. Long took over as Second Platoon leader. He would stay with us for six months and then go to battalion headquarters. That was the way it worked with the officers. I was glad to see him come and even sadder to see him go. We had been back to the company area for a time to get our equipment repaired and pick up some new guys. We did a few jobs around Long Bien, spending most nights at the club, which happened to be just across the field from our company area.

One night a few of us were at the club when a fight started, and before I knew it, most of the club was involved. We got under a table and kept drinking until the military police came, shutting the place down. I had started to isolate by now, going over to this little military police club to drink alone. They didn't like signal guys in there but left me alone because I never bothered anyone. I was just there to get drunk.

There was another time when the military police placed gun jeeps around the big club to break up a huge fight; we watched that one while sitting on top of our bunker sharing a bottle. We got a new platoon sergeant who was a Sergeant First Class E-7, and I have tried to remember his name for forty years and have not been able to. He was a good guy, with every one respecting him. Being an E-7, he had more clout with the first sergeant and battalion sergeant major.

The first mission we had under him was placing a cable underground outside the wire over by the ammo dump. When we got there, a sentry in one of the guard towers said he had been taking sniper fire since sunup, so the platoon sergeant told me and another guy to get out in the jungle a couple of hundred yards as flankers following the team as it moved along the road. He said if anything happened to fall back to his position.

I chambered a round and started to walk out into the bush when I heard this guy begging not to go. He was one of the older guys age-wise in the platoon, with a wife and kids back in the States. In his mind's eye, if he went out there, he was never going to see them again. I asked the platoon sergeant to let me take one of the other men, but he said no way and ordered the guy to get his butt out there. You could see the fear in his eyes, so I told him to stay behind me and if anything happened to take off in the other direction while I covered him. The sniper slipped away to come again another day, and we never received another round. When the job was done, that was one happy guy to get back to the main part of the platoon.

Another time a couple of us were sitting on a dirt mound watching the VC drop rockets and mortars into the same ammo dump when it looked like the whole damn place went up. You could see the shockwave as it came toward us so we concentrated our attention on the company mess hall, which was full of guys eating. When the shockwave hit, there were guys running through the walls. There was a lot of power and noise in that shockwave.

We left shortly after that for Can Tho in the Mekong Delta. Whenever we stayed there it was with the

Fifty-Second Signal Battalion located at the Can Tho Airfield, which was about four miles outside the city. We were never more than a platoon-sized force, so they gave us the bottom of one of their billets. Most of my drinking down there was done on the airfield. There was something about the city of Can Tho at night that I didn't like so I stayed away from it.

Chapter 15

A two-month deployment was coming up for Thailand, and the platoon sergeant said most of the Second Platoon would be going. When the time came, they brought us back to the company area from the Mekong Delta, and on the first night back, we got in trouble with the first sergeant. He had just built a day room for the company and was extremely proud of it. We should have stayed out of there, but when you get drunk, stupid comes out.

Some of the guys put a bull's-eye on the wall and threw their knives into it. A couple of other guys got into a fight and destroyed some of the furniture. For some reason, I got into an argument with SP/4 Ron Novak with him going for his pistol. Some of the guys grabbed him as I went out the window.

The next morning we were all standing in front of the first sergeant, and he wasn't happy. After calling us every name in the book, he told us to get out of his sight before he shot us himself, so off we went to Thailand. I think Lt. Long and our platoon sergeant had a lot to do with us being allowed to go. We went to the air force base at Bien Hoa to catch a civilian flight to Bangkok, Thailand.

Around fifteen of us boarded the plane that night. The stewardess told us we could sit anywhere we wanted because there weren't many people on the flight. Then a jerk air force major made an announcement that all army personnel who had just boarded were to go to the back of the plane and remain there until the plane landed. Since we were all enlisted, there wasn't anything we could do but go to the back of the plane. I didn't think we smelled that bad, but maybe we did. The stewardess came back and apologized, but it wasn't her fault.

When we got to Bangkok, we were met by a lieutenant who told us we would spend the night in Bangkok and head out in the morning for Sattahip, which was down south on the gulf of Thailand. I could not believe the amount of drugs that were available as soon as we got off the plane. They even had them rolled in cigarettes that were in sealed packages. That night most of us headed out, exploring the city and the majority of us came down in the morning without our mustaches, which most of us had grown while we were in Vietnam. I think it had to do with some sort of rite of passage. We heard that Thai women didn't like mustaches, so like good drunken soldiers; we fixed the problem right quick.

The lieutenant in charge was from Company B, Fortieth Signal Battalion, which was located up at Ban Me Thuet in the highlands of Vietnam. He was a great guy and thought of the deployment as a two-month party when we got off work. We were attached to the Sattahip Signal Detachment for rations and billets. We slept in canvas tents put on wooden platforms about six inches off the ground. The only problem was the holes in the floor because you never knew what would crawl out of them at any given moment. I used to put my boots over the ones near my bed, hoping to stop any snakes.

Every morning we would find snakes that were run over the night before on the road. One guy went to town and brought back a stuffed king cobra that was coiled as if it were ready to strike. He called me over and told me to look in the bag on his bed, and it almost caused me to have a heart attack. At that time you could buy a Bengal tiger skin for around two or three hundred dollars.

The drugs and booze flowed so freely that it seemed like the whole country was either drunk or stoned—but maybe that was because of the company we kept after hours. When we got into the rural areas, the people were really good to us. The people in the towns and cities were what we had made them over time. It was a very beautiful country, and the people seemed like the Cambodians I had met before. There were warring nations in that area but also peaceful ones that just wanted to be left alone and live their lives. Sad to say, that was not the way it always turned out.

We were at Sattahip for a couple of weeks when they told us to get ready to head north to Udon Thani (Udorn), where we would be staying at an army security agency camp about five miles south of Udorn. I think we spent the night at Bangkok on the way up. The ASA camp had really nice facilities that looked new, and the barracks were two-story cement block buildings. After what we had been living in, it was like being back in the States. They put us by ourselves on the second floor of this building along the perimeter fence. We couldn't start work for a week because we had to wait for our equipment to catch up. In the meantime, exploring the town was our main function. There was an American air force base at Udorn that was running bombing and strafing missions into North Vietnam. It was a rather large base with the ASA Camp backing them up with intelligence they pulled out of the air waves.

On about the third night there, I was at a bowling alley when a young woman kept crying about losing her husband who had gone back to the States. He was an air force guy who had married her under Thai law and then left her in Thailand. She was a Cambodian, nineteen or twenty years old, and a very sweet girl, plus she was not hard on the eyes. Her name was Toy, and the name fit her perfectly.

Toy had come to Thailand to find work while getting away from what was going on in Cambodia. Prostitution was considered an honorable profession in Southeast Asia, and forty some years later it helped spread AIDS throughout the region. I spent every spare moment I had with her. She lived in one of the back allies in town, and I got lost almost every time I went to her hooch. She never believed I would be leaving in a month to go back to Vietnam. I wonder what she thought when I disappeared, never to be seen again. I hope she found a nice military guy to marry and made it to the States. She deserved a good life after all she had been through.

It was at Udorn that I started throwing up blood. I was on my knees in front of the porcelain throne one morning doing my ritual when this weird-looking stuff started to come up. I didn't know what it was and would not find out until many years later even though it happened often. I figured whatever I was throwing up wasn't meant to be in my stomach so I might as well get rid of it. It was just part of the price I paid.

We were sent up north to place new underground cable around the ASA camp and take down the old communication lines in the air. One night we were awakened by someone running through our barracks yelling that the Thai Cong, as he called them, had blown up some aircraft at the air force base and intelligence thought the Cong was coming through our area and might hit the base because it was ASA. Just then the alert siren went off so out the door we went.

They issued us individual weapons with two M-60 machine guns, but the sticking point was they wanted us to go on line with no ammo. They told us if we got hit, they would get the ammo to us in time. We told them in unison to kiss off and when they got serious to let us know. We headed for the barracks, looking back at this formation that was assembled under streetlights. If the Thai Cong had already set up they could have wiped out most of the camp that night. We had no problem with going on line, but we just didn't want them to tie our hands behind our backs. Luckily the Thai Cong never showed up, and the platoon got a good night's sleep.

Some of the men who worked at the Mars site told everyone to come over and they would set up calls back to the States for us. They did this by short wave and then hooked into the local telephone company closest to where you were calling in the States. A few of us went over, but I didn't have the patience to wait around for them to patch the call together. Besides, I wanted to see Toy instead of waiting for some stupid phone call. I knew Toy had cold beer on hand, and I wanted to be there with her. The other guys got their calls through and talked with their families back in the States. It just wasn't that important to me. Besides, I thought of my life as there, not back in the States.

Not long after that I was told to report to the Red Cross unit at the air base because they wanted to see me about something. When I got there, they informed me that there had been a request for information about me because no one had received any letters from me for a couple of months back in the States. They said I could call the States if I wanted to, but I told the Red Cross to let them know where I was and that I would write when I got back to Vietnam. That sounds cold, but it was the way it was.

The last night there we were at the club drinking, and the drunker I got, the meaner I got. Finally a sergeant came over and told me to keep it down or he would be forced to throw me out. I had just picked up a really juicy hamburger when he said that so I took off the top piece of bread and rubbed the rest of it onto the paneled wall. As I stumbled outside to the swimming pool, I told everyone that if they didn't like what I did I would be outside. That was one irate sergeant, but he also knew that we would be leaving in the morning with our final destination being back in 'Nam. I have no doubt he was hoping I got killed there. The only guy who came out was one of our guys, and he helped me back to the barracks.

The next morning we left at separate times, establishing a location where we would hook up once we got to Bangkok. Bob and I drove in a two-and-a-half-ton truck, with Bob taking a prostitute with him. Bob said he was taking her to Bangkok so she didn't have to pay bus fare. I didn't care one way or the other because I was still hung over from the night before. Bob started to drive, but after a while he thought it was time for me to take over, and he told me to grab the wheel. I slid over and the woman climbed onto my lap. As Bob went out the driver's door, I slid into the driver's seat, and he made his way over the back of the truck, coming in the passenger's door. This was done while we drove down the highway at about fifty miles an hour. We changed places a few times on the way to Bangkok, while the local Thai drivers laughed and shook their heads at us. We came upon an accident where a guy was laying alongside the road with his head almost cut off. There was nothing we could do, so we kept going down the road.

We hooked up with the rest of the platoon at a hotel and made plans for the night. All our rooms were on the seventh floor, and the quickest way to get them cool was to crank open the windows, which went out beyond a one-and-a-half-foot ledge, wrapping around the building. One of the guys bet me a beer I wouldn't go out on the ledge so I had to prove how stupid I was. All of the windows were cranked out, so to get on the other side, I would grab the top of the window and swing myself around it. It took a couple of windows before I looked down at the hotel pool, thinking just maybe I could jump and make it into the water. Thank God a little bit of sanity returned and I got my butt back on the right side of the wall.

One guy bought a bag of weed and then climbed into this hotel closet. We taped all the cracks around the doors shut, and he stayed inside for most of the time we were there. The bag was empty when he floated out. The same guy tried to chew off Sgt. Hawks big toe a couple of nights later after he got drunk and went nuts. Hawks was so drunk that he let him chew on it while he drank his beer. The guy was shipped back to 'Nam the next day and then sent to the Mekong Delta.

It was a good time in Thailand, and we took advantage of all it had to offer. I don't remember doing much work when we got back to Sattahip. We went to town every night, and one guy always drank a bottle of Listerine before he went. Said it was cheaper that way. I never went on R&R (rest and relaxation) while I was in Vietnam. I spent two months in Thailand, and what could be better than that?

Four of us went to the Gulf of Thailand one afternoon to drink some beer and relax. After a couple of hours, some Thai guys showed up, so we sat around drinking a few with them. Finally it became clear that something wasn't right as pistols started to appear. The guys still seemed friendly so we didn't think too much about it, but we decided it would be better to be out of there before it got dark.

When it came time for us to go back to Vietnam, we spent one more night in Bangkok. One of the guys from our platoon had fallen in love with a woman who had a young son and swore up and down he was going to send her the money to go to the States and wait for him. Then they would get married after he got back from Vietnam. I never did hear how that one turned out, but it sure sounded crazy to the rest of us. At the airbase we loaded up in the back of a C-130 cargo plane, and it was the noisiest thing I have ever been on. I sure was glad to get on the ground at Bien Hoa.

Chapter 16

Lt. Long kept a couple of extra cases of c-rations on hand in case we had to leave unexpectedly in the middle of the night, which we did at times. One night two of us stole the c-rations, and it took a couple of days for us to finish them off. When the lieutenant discovered they were missing, he called the platoon together, telling us he had signed out for them and now he had to pay for them and he hoped the scumbags who stole them got food poisoning. To this day I think he knew I was somehow involved with it but never said anything. We went to the captain and confessed to taking them so the lieutenant wouldn't have to pay. We liked him and didn't want him taking crap over something as stupid as c-rations.

Shortly after we got back from Thailand, Lt. Long told Bix and me to be ready to head for Can Tho the next morning because the guys were getting in trouble there and we would be going to help him get things straightened out. We jumped on a chopper the next morning, and away we went. When we got there, the guys had grenades hanging in their lockers with ammo lying all over, and the place was a mess. There was also a major argument going on with some people in another unit at the air strip, and death threats had been made. It took a couple of days and some major butt chewing before everything was put in order. To celebrate what a great job we did, we went to the club and had more than our share of Mr. Jim Beam.

At about ten o'clock that night, the guys asked me to take them to town. I didn't want to because the road was dangerous at night, but you have to take care of your buddies. We got a three-quarter-ton truck loaded up and headed off into the night. How we ever got out of the front gate is beyond me. I dropped them off at a bar and drove a little further into town. I went around what used to be a huge water fountain but had become a reinforced bunker manned by South Vietnam forces. After waving at them, I headed back toward the air strip, only to see the military police had already picked up the guys I had just dropped off. I didn't think that was right so I pulled over to where they were and tried to con the military police into releasing my buddies, promising they would be dealt with most severely when we got back to the air strip. This coming out of a guy who was three sheets to the wind.

The military police thought that was a bad idea and suggested I turn over my weapon and join my buddies on their way to jail. There we were in the military police station when Lt. Long came through the door, and was he ticked. He got us released, telling Bix and me to get into the back of his jeep. He chewed on us all the way back to the air strip, saying if we didn't get in the gate he would shoot us himself. I was never so glad to see that gate swing open. We both knew the lieutenant was mad enough to do it. It was never brought up after that night, but I'll bet he has told the story a few times over the years. His family owned a telephone company in Georgia, and he asked Bix and me to think about working for them when we got out. For some reason the lieutenant liked us. He let some things slide that could have gotten us in trouble. I think that is what made him a good leader. He always completed the mission but at the same time took care of his men the best he could.

On September 6, 1968, twelve of us were attached to the Fifty-Second Signal Battalion at Can Tho in the Mekong Delta. Lt. Long rotated to battalion headquarters. Our new lieutenant came down in a convoy to meet us and spend time finding out how things worked. While he was there, he had steel plates welded on his jeep so it looked like a traveling tank. He also tried to bring state-side regulations to our platoon, which didn't sit well with us. We had no problem doing whatever we needed to stay alive and get the mission done, but we didn't need someone to tell us to shine our boots and have starched fatigues. After a couple weeks of this, we were sitting in our hooch drinking a few beers when he came in and sat down. We offered him a beer, and awhile later he pulled out pictures of his wife and kids. I don't remember who said it, but he came to understand that if he kept up the crap, his wife was going to be a widow. He turned out to be almost as good as Lt. Long.

It was during this trip to the Delta that Bix talked me into staying in town all night. I have no idea why I said yes, but I did. We got dropped off at about six o'clock at night in front of this bar we knew. Pretty soon we had eaten and drank ourselves into a mellow mood. Bix said he was going upstairs with one of the prostitutes and would see me in the morning. I had a couple of more beers and then decided which one I wanted to spend the night with, so up the stairs we went.

Sometime during the night I heard a gun battle taking place in the alley below my second-floor window. The girl I was with was whispering VC in my ear as I grabbed my weapon, heading to the window. There were six of them moving along the alley while they were engaged in a firefight with Korean civilians who lived off the alley. You have to love those Koreans. There was no sense in letting them know I was there because the Koreans were taking care of the situation. After the firefight died down, I went back to bed and slept till morning. That was the last time I slept in town. Have I mentioned that people do the stupidest things when they drink? How do you think that would have been written up in the hometown paper? Sp/4 Phil Spencer was killed the other night in South Vietnam while trapped in a whorehouse by a squad of Vietcong. What an epitaph!

We were placing cable across the Song Hau Giang River one day, and I was in a cable car riding the strand. A cable car is something you sit on with rollers at the top, and you pull yourself along the steel strand the cable is attached to. This river was so wide that once you got to the middle, there was no way you were going to pull yourself to the other side. The guys threw me a pull rope because I was only about twenty feet from the side of the bridge, and then they told me they were going to get something to eat and for me to hang in there. I cussed them up one side and down the other as they drove off.

When I had been hanging there for about ten minutes, a guy came out of the woods dressed in black pajamas, an AK-47 and VC equipment and started to walk across the bridge. No one else on the bridge seemed to notice, but I couldn't take my eyes off him. I had no weapon on me. The thought of going into the river wasn't appealing, but I knew I would have to if he drew down on me. I had already unhooked my safety strap in case it came to that. When he got to the other side of the bridge and disappeared back into the woods, I took a deep breath and realized I wasn't going to die that day. I found out later he was a road runner working for the Green Berets. When the guys got back they thought it was the funniest thing they had heard in a long time, but that was the last time I went into a cable car.

I came wide awake one night at the airfield to small arms fire and explosions going off. The VC came through the front gate in a stolen ambulance, going up one side of the flight line and then down the other, throwing satchel charges. They blew up some aircraft, and if I remember right, they drove back out the front gate.

Later in the month I was stringing wire across the roof of a police station just down the road from the river when I heard a horrific scream coming from the road. I was about twenty feet off the ground and thirty feet from the shoulder of the road. I turned just in time to see a woman who was about thirty years old get caught up in the rear dual tires of a five thousand-gallon tanker truck. Everything slowed down as her upper body went between the rear dual tires. She was screaming until the tires ran over her, and then somehow she got caught in them, going around three or four more times. Her arms, legs, and head were flopping as the tires tore her apart. When she did come out the back, there wasn't much left. Traffic had stopped completely on the crowded road, and it seemed like no one was moving to help when someone from a car picked up what was left of the body, threw her in the backseat, and headed down the road. There was a lot of her left on the road, and the unfairness of it was overwhelming. I had seen violent death before, but for some reason this wasn't right. I didn't know it at the time, but this would come back to bite me later in life.

In November we went back to the company area, and I was getting close to rotating back to the States. On Thanksgiving Day of 1968 we were told we could go to the air force base for turkey and all the trimmings. We loaded up a three-quarter-ton truck and headed out. As we pulled up to the main gate, I told the driver to stop because I was going into town instead and to pick me up on the way out. Before I could go I had to cut a cast off my leg so I wouldn't be stopped by the military police because you could not be in town with a cast on. I'm not sure why I had the cast on, but I knew it had to come off if I wanted to go to the bars. They went to the chow hall and got food poisoning from bad turkey while I got drunk downtown.

Shortly after the trip to the air base, our platoon sergeant gave me orders where I was reassigned to Fort Bragg, North Carolina, but while he did this, he also suggested I should extend my tour in Vietnam. He went on to explain that Fayetteville, North Carolina was not a good match for my personality and at least I could carry a weapon in 'Nam. I thought about it for five seconds and told him to draw up the papers to extend my tour. I guess he had the same conversation with Bix because he extended also.

When Lieutenant Long heard what we had done, he came looking for us. He wanted to know if we had totally lost our minds. He was leaving at about the same time, and it was as if he wanted to make sure we left there in one piece. Like I said, he was a good officer, always looking out for his men.

The platoon adopted one of the cooks at the company area because whenever we came back, he was always ready to drink and join us when we got into trouble, and he always gave us extra chow. He was shipped to another company up north, and we heard that he was killed when his camp was overrun. Just before I left to go back to the States on leave, we were at the company area watching a movie on the outdoor screen sharing a few beers. It was a foggy night when who should walk around the corner of the movie screen but the cook. We looked at one another as if we were seeing a ghost. When we realized he wasn't a ghost, we rushed the guy, hugging him and telling him how great it was to see him. He told us when they were overrun he had been hit and spent time in the hospital but went back to the camp after he recovered. He too was getting ready to go back to the States.

Chapter 17

On December 2, 1968, I received orders for thirty days of leave time back in the States. This was one of the benefits when you extended your tour, and I also got a month taken off the time I had to stay in the army. Once again I had a lot of money saved up, and the party began when I stepped off the plane. I hooked up with Gary Eastwell, who in turn took me over to where Kay Zimmerman and Cherri Sierocki lived. Cherri and I hit it off. We stayed pretty close while I was home and also for a while when I got out of the army. Cherri had transferred to Freeland High School after I was thrown out so we had never met.

We ate at their place one night, and instead of using a fork, I reached into the salad bowl with my hand and took out what I wanted. Kay glanced my way, and you could tell from her expression she wasn't used to being around someone who would do that. It was the way I had lived for years, and for me it was normal. The whole month was a drunken blur as I used and abused people. It's amazing how you think you're having such a great time with everyone being your buddy, but the next morning you can't remember crap because the whole night turned into a blackout and all your so-called buddies are gone, along with your money.

I started writing this standing at the back of the Methodist church so I will continue the story from there. I don't know how long I stood there wondering why I had come out on the short end of life, but I knew I had. There was nothing left to do but continue to go in the same direction because that was all I knew. It was sad but in a way comforting for I knew how to survive this way. Besides, I didn't have the strength or wisdom to change. I turned and walked out into the snow, not looking back, for I believed there was nothing there for me.

On my last night before going back to 'Nam I was drinking at Roeditcher's bar when the daughter of a guy I knew came in. I ask her how her dad was, and she replied we could go see him if I wanted, so away we went. My brother, who happened to be drunk on my dime, thought I should be spending the night differently, and when I got back to the bar, he yanked me out of the car through the window. I could have taken him out with a shot to the groin or throat but you don't do that to your brother, so I let him take his shot and got my nose broke. The guys back at the platoon thought it was hilarious.

The next morning was foggy with no planes leaving, so Cherri said she would drive me the two hours down to Detroit to catch a plane for Oakland, California. She was sick at the time, and even in the shape I was in, I felt sorry for her. She had an aunt who lived down there, so she spent the night with her. It took the better part of two days before I fully sobered up.

I spent three days at Oakland, and then the army loaded us on a plane, and off we went to sunny Vietnam. It was interesting to watch the cherries (new guys) on the plane. You could see their bewilderment and apprehension.

When we were getting ready to touch down the VC sent us a welcome back present. The plane was probably a couple hundred feet above the runway when mortars started to land. The pilot went full throttle with those four big jets just a-screaming. The plane was swaying from side to side as we climbed out of range. The pilot circled the field a couple of times and then brought us in for a safe landing. The adrenaline was rushing, but at the same time, the thought came that just maybe I had made a mistake and Lt. Long had been right. It took a few days to get my mind-set to where it needed to be. Other than the time I was caught in the whorehouse, I had never before thought I might die in Vietnam.

It was good to be back with the platoon because I had missed them. I was closer to them than my blood family. It's hard to explain, but if you've been through it, you know what I'm saying. Two of us were picked to take some material down to Quan Long where some of the platoon was. We caught a ride on a C-7 Caribou, and as it took off, I reached for the butt can. Yeah, back then you could smoke on airplanes. As I reached for the can, I realized someone from the previous flight must have thrown up in it because it slid out of my hand with all that warm puke going down the front of me. Needless to say, everyone moved away from me at this point. When I got to Can Tho I used sand to clean off as much as I could and then put my clothes back on because that was all I had to wear.

We caught a chopper from Can Tho to Quan Long, getting there late in the day. It was a pretty town. I believe it was this town that looked like a scene from one of the Vietnam movies they made in the 1980s. A small river ran through the town, with hanging lanterns for light and a cement arched bridge that you could only walk over. We were only there a couple of days and then headed back to the company area. We had caught a chopper at the local air strip and were skimming along at treetop level with two warrant officers sitting across from us. We asked them if they were going to pick up a chopper or what when they told us the one we were on was their bird. They started to laugh, telling us the door gunner and crew chief were flying the chopper. Those two guys were very good at flying so we kicked back and enjoyed the scenery.

When we got to Can Tho, there weren't any more flights out that day, so we were stuck, and since none of our platoon was there, we spent the night sleeping on a cement pad at the airstrip. There were some guys who had just gotten in country, wearing shiny new uniforms. They were waiting for a flight the next morning. You could tell they were nervous, and wouldn't you know, someone started to fire at the end of the runway. These guys were hiding behind anything they could, and then one of them popped a round off, shooting down the runway. We let them know in no uncertain terms that if they did it again, the VC would be the least of their worries. We enlightened them to the fact that there were bunkers on the perimeter at the end of the runway and they were shooting at our own men. There were also helicopters, C-7 Caribous, and some C-130s down the flight line, and the last thing you wanted to do was put a bullet in one of them. We told them to lie down and go to sleep, and if the VC made it onto the airfield, we would know soon enough. I don't know if they went to sleep, but we did. The next morning we flew back to Bien Hoa air base, catching a ride to the company area.

By now racial tension from the States had come to Vietnam. We had a black guy named Junior in my platoon who kept me from being pulled off a pole by a steel messenger strand. There is no way I would be alive if it had not been for him that day. We were on opposite sides of the pole when a truck hit the steel strand I had laying on my belt. It rode up my body, and just before it hit my neck, I turned my head so it didn't hook under my chin, taking my head off, but instead rode up the side of my face. Junior reached out, grabbing me as I started to go down the pole. If he hadn't done that, there is no doubt I would have gone off the pole that day.

Junior went home on special leave a short time later, but when he came back, something had changed him while he was in the States. This was in the late sixties, so it's hard to say what it was, but he would have nothing to do with any of the white guys in the platoon when he came back. He was the same as a brother to me and always will be. Wherever you are, man, I hope life has treated you well.

The only time I saw racism was when we were back at the company area. It was late in my second tour. That was also true with drugs because only a few guys in our platoon played with them. We had one kid who loved his dope, spending time in the Long Bien jail because of it. He had a wild plan for how to get a large quantity of dope into the States. We told him he was nuts, but he wouldn't listen. He left for the States a couple of months before me. When you got to the Oakland army terminal, they would give you one chance to get rid of anything you should not have. After that if they found anything, you belonged to them. Guess what I saw sitting there as an example of what guys used to smuggle stuff in? It was the container that the guy from our company had used to try and get his dope into the States. They caught the guy, but I never did hear how much time he got. Imagine that—a druggie wasn't as smart as he thought he was.

I spent the rest of my time in the Mekong Delta until it was time to head back to the States. During the last couple of weeks, we were brought back and given jobs around the company area. They gave me the job of water truck driver, which involved driving a five-ton tractor with a five thousand-gallon tanker on the back supplying water for the company. About a week later, I got it stuck between two buildings and could not get it out of there. It would not go forward or backward, so I shut it off and went looking for the first sergeant, telling him what had happened and that I didn't think I was cut out for the job. He called me a few choice names and then put me on another job until it was time for me to process out. One of the things the first sergeant was good at was ripping you a new one, which seemed like he did every time he met anyone from the Second Platoon.

When I got to the Ninetieth Replacement Battalion, I did something I have regretted ever since. We were waiting for the bus that was going to take us to the plane when I was bumped from the flight by someone who was going home on special leave. It happened to be a guy from my company who had lost his mother and was going back for the funeral. I went off on the poor guy with a rage that was as hot as it could get. All I could think about was getting killed during that extra night I was going to spend in country while not giving a crap what this guy was going through. Insanity is never far off and appears whenever it wants to. If you're out there man I'm sorry.

I made it through the night, catching the first flight out of Vietnam the following morning. When I got to Oakland, I believe the processing out took a couple of days. It was July 6, 1969, when I was released from active duty, and on July 7, 1969, I was discharged and assigned to Standby United States Army Reserve Control Group. It had been five years, two months, and twenty-two days since I was a civilian, and I really wasn't sure how to act in what we called the real world.

Chapter 18

When I arrived in Michigan, I moved in with my grandparents for a while, soon to make their lives miserable with my constant drinking. I stayed drunk for the first two weeks, spreading my type of joy wherever I went. About a week after I came back from 'Nam, I was talking to my dad's older sister, and for some reason, she slapped me. To this day I don't know why, but if it hadn't been for Grandpa standing next to us at the time, his daughter would have died that day. My hands were going for her throat as Grandpa screamed at me to get out of there, forcing himself between us. She stayed away from me after that. I didn't have any use for her before, but after that I downright disliked her.

I was in Freeland drinking with some of the guys when I was asked a question that stopped me in my tracks: how did it feel to kill someone? Having a little too much beer in me, I made some off-handed remark, trying to make a joke out of it. But it shocked me to my very core that someone would ask that. They not only had no understanding of death but also in my opinion had no understanding of life. I've had other combat vets tell me they felt the same way when asked that question. What I should have said was, "Why don't you get off your butt, go to the closest military recruiting office, volunteer for Vietnam, go over, and find out for yourself?" The guy who asked me that had never been in the military to my knowledge.

I have been asked that question a few times over the years, and every time it shocks me. Never has another veteran asked me that, only dumb civilians who never looked at service to their country as something that was owed it. The one thing I know for sure is that being a politician is not serving your country. They love to imply it is, but the only things they serve are their egos.

Then you have the wannabes who say they were never in the military, but if they had been, they would have volunteered for Vietnam. These are the same guys who did everything possible to get out of it. The thing that irritates veterans, and especially combat veterans, is if they say they would have gone then why didn't they? I knew a guy at the very end of my working career who told me that, and from then on I had nothing but contempt for him. There were good men dying in the jungles and rice paddies of Vietnam when this puke was in the backseat of his daddy's car playing with someone else's girlfriend. It's easy to shoot your mouth off about what you would have done knowing you will never have to prove it. There were a lot of men who were drafted and went to Vietnam, coming home either in a body bag, not at all, or with parts missing. For these worthless pieces of scum to even hint that they are of the same caliber dishonors all who served and died for this country.

It took over twenty years of reading books and looking back on my own experience in Vietnam for me to come to a simple conclusion: I don't think of Vietnam as a war but as a campaign in a war. The American military did some amazing things there even with one hand tied behind its back. We held up Russia and China for over ten years so they couldn't do other things they wanted to. We lost Vietnam because of stupid politicians, but we won the Cold War in spite of them.

I was asked what I thought of Muhammad Ali when he refused to go into the military. He stood up for what he believed and paid the consequences for it. I respect anyone who stands up for their convictions but not the slime balls who didn't go and now in some way want to be part of it. And don't even get me started on the ones who went to Canada. The stereotype that Hollywood and the news media gave us of being drug-crazed baby killers was a bunch of crap, and they should hang their heads in shame for what they did to disgrace the Vietnam veterans in the eyes of the public.

I have had people tell me they didn't want Vietnam veterans around their children and families or have them in the workplace because they were crazy and could not be trusted. The ones who can't be trusted are the idiot politicians who sent us and are still sending people to fight in wars the politicians started through their own stupidity. I think the one prerequisite for being a politician is a lack of common sense because none of them seem to have any.

When the medals stop being shiny
When the ribbons are torn and tattered
When the memories start to fade
Remember
Some saw it on television
Some listened to it on the radio

Some read about it in books and magazines
But you did none of these
You didn't have to because you were there
You lived it
You breathed it
You fought it
It is a part of you that will last until
The day you die
—Author Unknown

When I came back from Vietnam in July of 1969, Mom had been sober for a couple of months. She asked what I missed most while in Vietnam and I told her fried pork chops, so that's what we ate every time I went there for the next couple of months. They were living in a nice trailer park south of Saginaw on Dixie Highway. Duane would have a beer with me, but he had cut way back on his drinking. They were both happy, and life seemed to be smiling on them. Grandma Brewster was living with them at the time, and they seemed to be enjoying life. After a time Mom told me I should look at my drinking before it got away from me like it had with her. If only she knew how much I was drinking she would have been more concerned.

I was sitting at a bar in Freeland one night when a guy I knew from school came in and sat down next to me. He had been one of the high school jocks and apparently thought he still was. For no reason he told me I should watch myself because they had a really tough police department in town and he didn't want to see me get in trouble. It seemed weird because I hadn't been in trouble, and why would he think I would be? I hadn't seen him in five and a half years. He didn't know me from Adam, but nonetheless I said thanks and bought him a beer. Come to find out he was on the police department and was playing tough guy at my expense. If he knew the men I had been with and would have died for only a few weeks before he would have kept his mouth shut and realized that both he and his police department would have been the least of my worries. Human ego is a strange thing. It's so fragile and constantly needs to puff itself up.

A little while later I was in Midland at about one o'clock in the morning, trying to navigate my way back to Freeland after a night of bar hopping. I don't know if I saw the lights first or heard the siren, but the city police had snuck up on my tail. It might have been that they saw me weaving all over the road, but I was in luck because it happened that I was less than a block away from a church where my sister and brother-in-law lived, so I continued down the road with the police following me with their lights on. I pulled around to the back of the church and staggered out of the car.

They started to ask the normal questions, but they knew I was as drunk as a skunk. I told them I was trying to make it to my sister's house to spend the night, which they didn't believe. About that time Don and Carol came out of their apartment, asking what was going on. The officers asked them if they knew me, and once they said yes, the police left me in their custody telling me if they saw me again that night I was going to jail. That was another problem I got out of but should have gone to jail over.

I had met a married couple through Butch and Sue the last time I was home. They were living at Central Michigan University, where he was going to school, while his wife worked at Dow Chemical Company with Sue. I decided one Saturday that I would go see them, so I drove the twenty miles from Midland to Mt. Pleasant. After spending an afternoon of drinking, we decided to go see *They Shoot Horses, Don't They?* that was playing at the movie theatre. At the end of the movie, the main character takes a pistol, holds it to the side of their head, and pulls the trigger. The whole theater gasped at the realization of how this movie had just ended. To me it was the funniest thing I had seen in a long time, and I laughed all the way out of the theater. Remember, I had only been out of 'Nam for about three weeks. Needless the say, those college students didn't understand my sense of humor.

On the way back to Freeland, I once again got pulled over by the police, only this time the Michigan State Police had me. It was about nine o'clock at night, and I was in a hurry to get back so I could get to the bars and see what I could pick up. There were two officers, and they had me get out of the car while asking what was going on. I wasn't really drunk yet but had enough in me that I would have failed a field sobriety test. I told them where I was coming from and going and that I had just gotten back from Vietnam about three weeks before. They took pity on me and let me off, telling me to watch my driving a little closer and to get off the road as soon as I got to Freeland. One more missed opportunity to possibly get Phil headed in the right direction.

Twenty-one days after I was discharged from the army, I was hired at AT&T as a pole lineman at Midland, Michigan. I put in over thirty-eight years before retiring from the digital operation group in Racine, Wisconsin. As I look back on it, the time I spent in the line crews was the most rewarding. Everything you did after that was because you could no longer perform real work. Shortly after starting work, we went on a nationwide strike. I walked the picket line drunk or on my way to getting there. They talk about big strikes today of fifty thousand people. When we walked out, over seven hundred and fifty thousand people walked out the door. Ma Bell, as it was called, was the biggest employer around.

When we finally got back to work, I was hanging on a pole listening to these test center guys talking among themselves when one asked the other if he had seen those two scummy-looking dirt bags that had just been hired in the line crew. Then said something about how this country must be hard up to have veterans who looked like that. One of the guys was me, and the other a marine (who had long hair) that had been hired about the same time. I told him I was one of those dirt bags and asked if he wanted me to come up to his test center and rearrange his face.

It got real silent at the other end of the line, and then it went dead. After that we called the second-level supervisor, filling him in while letting him know what we were going to do. He told us not to do anything because he would personally take care of it. He was a man of his word because nobody said anything about Vietnam veterans after that. We went over there, putting our lives on the line, and this moron said something like that. A lot of the men who served in Vietnam were drafted, not being there by choice, but they did the job demanded of them with honor and then came home, only to be kicked in the teeth and stabbed in the back not only by their countrymen but sometimes also by members of their own families.

I found out over time that was the way most of the country felt about us, including a lot of WWII and Korean veterans. There were some VFW and American Legion Halls that wouldn't acknowledge we were even in combat. No wonder most Vietnam veterans told them to kiss off, not having anything to do with them until years later. I became a life member of the VFW thirty-five years later but have never gone to a meeting. I joined the American Legion later in Marquette only to be able to drink at their bar.

By then I was starting to have flashbacks fairly often, and guilt was setting in for leaving my buddies in 'Nam. There were long, sleepless nights with moments of terror, remorse, and total confusion. There were night sweats, and unknown fear constantly ripped me apart. I didn't like the dark, and even to this day I sleep with some sort of night light. I hated the way the war was being covered and the way my so-called countrymen treated the returning veterans. I started to bury it, and the longer I worked at it, the deeper it became buried. The only time it was manageable was when I was drunk or on my way to getting drunk. I was self-medicating myself and didn't know it.

The breaking point for me came one night as I sat in a Freeland bar. Al Hinkle came in, just having returned from 'Nam. We were sitting at a table having a beer when he started to bring up some of the things he did over there. My mind slammed shut, not opening up for a very long time where Vietnam was concerned. I told him I couldn't go there anymore and walked out of the bar. When I hit the fresh air outside, I leaned up against the side of the building, shaking like a leaf in a windstorm. It took some time for the shaking to go away, and the feeling of being alone was totally overwhelming. In my mind I had no place to turn, no place to hide, and no one to cover my back. The only thing I knew to do was drink, and with that came the relief I sought.

A couple of weeks later, I was driving from the old man's house back to Freeland on a rural road when a van pulled up alongside me, and it was full of guys I knew. They had been drinking and driving around the countryside and asked if I wanted to join them. I took the car back to my dad's and left with them in the van. We had been driving around most of the afternoon drinking when the neighborhood bully started to run his mouth about something. We got into an argument, so I picked up a handsaw in the back of the van, figuring I would use it on his neck, when the other guys got in between us.

The tears started to come as all I could think of was killing this piece of scum. I know the other people in the van had not a clue what was going on in my mind at the time. They must have figured it would be good to get me out of there because they headed for my dad's house. As I went to get out of the side door, the same scumbag kicked me from behind, and I went head first into a drainage ditch filled with water. As I lay in the ditch, the whole van erupted in laughter.

A feeling I hadn't experienced since 'Nam started to build, and all I wanted was to see dead bodies. I was as drunk as a skunk but still got in my car and started after the van, but they must have turned off somewhere because I never caught up with them. I can't remember if I had my P-38 in the glove box that day but I had the car and knew I could take them out with that. The old man followed me to Freeland, telling me later I ran two stop signs, almost hitting cars and driving like an insane man. It wasn't about driving for me at that moment; it was about killing everyone in that van.

There is no way I would ever treat a veteran the way they did me, drunk or sober, and to do it to a combat veteran makes it even more despicable. I put myself into a position where alcohol was in control of not only me but also the situation, and as usual, alcohol had its way. It's a terrible thing to realize you no longer have a home, country, or anyone you can rely on. The only ones I could rely on were back in Vietnam, and in my mind, I had deserted them.

Chapter 19

I started to see the younger sister of my brother's wife. Her name was Peggy Simmerman, and for some reason she thought it would be a good idea to be with me. I had moved out of Freeland and was living at Midland in a duplex. After we became engaged, AT&T had a company party we went to, and wouldn't you know, this guy had moonshine he was sharing. I took a few swigs out of the jar, and that is all I remember. They say later that night I took Peg's engagement ring and threw it out into the front yard. It took them about an hour to find it in the dark. Later I passed out on the couch with a cigarette in my hand, which caused my shirt to catch on fire. It's a miracle I didn't burn the apartment down.

On August 14, 1970, we were married, and there might have been twenty people who came. Her parents were not happy she was marrying me because of what they perceived had happened between me and the middle daughter. Since they were mad to begin with, there was no one invited from their side of the family. Her brother, Larry, was my best man. He had just returned from Vietnam, where he had been decorated for bravery. Like me he brought back some of Vietnam with him.

I remember one time he brought a girl to our apartment, and I told him to wake me up when they left so I could lock the door. He was just starting to bend over to wake me when I went for his throat. He was a hair quicker than me, having just come back from 'Nam, and managed to get out of my way in time.

Grandma and Grandpa Spencer didn't come for it seems I must have said something that ticked them off. I have no idea what it was, but everyone has their own choices to make. The parents of one of Peg's friends had a party for us so there was beer to be had. The party was just down the road from Butch and Sue's house so everyone was going back and forth all night. Butch was still drinking at the time so he had more than his share. He and Larry got into it; with Larry hitting him so hard in the chest I thought he broke some ribs. One thing about Larry—he didn't take crap off anybody.

Peg and I left the next morning, going to the Upper Peninsula for a week. That was only the second time in my life I had been there so it was interesting to me. Peg's relatives lived in a little town called McMillian just west of Newberry in the Upper Peninsula. I got along best with Bill and Eleanor because they liked to drink and their house was next to a bar. I would do a lot of drinking in that bar over the course of the next couple of years. When we got back to Midland, the stupidity continued, with me thinking it was normal. After my childhood and over five years in the military, I had no idea what normal was, but thought I did. Looking back on the marriage, it never stood a chance with my drinking and insanity going full steam ahead.

In the summer of 1971, Peg and I were at home watching television one night when a Billy Graham crusade came on. At the end of the program where they say the sinner's prayer, we got on our knees in front of the television and said it with him. There will be people within the religious community who would say I didn't mean it because of the life I led afterward, but they would be wrong. I meant every word, but sad to say, I didn't know what to do to follow up on it. The thought of finding a church and going to it never entered my mind. I believed I said the prayer from my heart and meant what I said, and it was up to Jesus to do the rest, whatever that might be.

We went to bed mad at each other one night, and during the night I had a flashback and drilled Peg right between the eyes with a left hook. She wasn't too happy about that, but I did not do it intentionally. There was one instance, though, when I smacked her around while we lived in Midland. There could have been more, but if there was I don't remember. Peg and a friend of hers came out to her brother's late one night to see what was going on. I was supposed to be staying there all night, but when they showed up, I decided to go back with her.

As usual I was really messed up and in a foul mood. When we got into town I was in the backseat of the car, and for some reason I started to hit her from behind, calling her every name in the book. She slammed on the brakes and bailed out of the car. She and her friend took off running down the road, screaming at me to stay away from them. Somehow I got the car to the duplex, passing out on the floor. I came to the next morning, and Peg was looking through the window, asking if it was okay to come in. I never knew when the beast would come out, but when he did, there was no stopping him until he had totally had his way.

Another time Larry and I were sitting in our living room passing a fifth of whiskey back and forth when Peg said something I didn't like. I yelled at her as she was going into another room, and when she turned around, I threw the whiskey bottle at her head, missing her by inches. I threw it so hard it actually broke the plaster and lath board on the wall. Why she didn't leave me right then is a mystery. She would have saved herself a lot of misery if she had.

There was a married couple we hung with who were into nudity, and when you got around them, the clothes usually came off. The guy must have taken nude pictures of every female in our group and then some. I saw his collection one time and was amazed at all the local women who were in it. I asked how he talked them into it, he said he would just come right out asking if they wanted to pose nude, with most of them saying yes. Then there were other couples who were into swinging, and things would get crazy when we were with them. We never got involved even though I tried to talk her into it at times. I had missed out on the sixties because of the military so I figured why not. It was a crazy time back then. It seemed like even the so-called normal people had their own quirks. They just hid it better from society than the alcoholics and drug addicts.

The first winter we were married the line crew went to work out of town about thirty miles away in Gladwin. They put us up in a motel with an expense account so it was nothing more than a great big party when we got off work. I was sitting at the motel one night drinking when I called up my mother's brother. I had heard he had said things about how Carol and I would end up. I called him every name in the book and then some. I would go back to Midland on Friday nights and then head back on Sunday night.

It was in Gladwin that I had my first adulterous affair in the marriage, but it would not be the last. I was an unrestrained animal when it came to what my body sought, caring only about my own gratification and drinking as much booze as I could. The emotional consequences the next morning were horrible, but by mid-afternoon I could not wait to start again. I never fell asleep or woke up while on the road; it was always passing out and coming to. Even on the nights when I didn't drink (which were few) I would close my eyes from exhaustion because of what I had done the night before. We worked out of town most of that winter, and up until I got out of the line crews, I always spent winters on the road, taking down old cable that had been replaced the summer before. Peg found out about the affair when I got drunk and told her. There was trouble in the house for a long time after that.

About a year and a half into the marriage, we made the decision to move to the Upper Peninsula of Michigan. I called it a decision at the time, but it really was a geographic change. I put in a transfer, hoping to get close to Escanaba, but we eventually went to Ironwood, which sits on the border with Wisconsin across the river from Hurley. I could not find a place in Ironwood to rent, finally finding a second-floor apartment in an old house in Wakefield. The man who owned it was eighty-three years old and had a habit of walking into the apartment whenever he wanted to. After he did this a few times, I put a lock on the inside of the door that he didn't have a key for. He was a nice guy, letting me park our car in an old garage he had on the property. I remember when Peg first saw the apartment she started to cry because there wasn't anything in it. We had to buy all the appliances and some floor cabinets for storage. We became friends with a young couple across the street, and Peg and the wife of one of the guys I worked with would get together every now and then.

It was during the time we spent in Wakefield that I had my first encounters with delirium tremors (DTs). Peg had gone to a women's party, and I started to drink as soon as she was out the door. I had a full fifth of whiskey and by ten o'clock that was down to a third of a bottle. I remember being on my knees in front of the porcelain throne and throwing up until I thought my stomach was coming out. With each dry heave, this shark would come out of the commode, trying to bite my head off. It was good I had some whiskey left because I was able to drink myself out of the DTs. I sure did hate it when I had them even though they were not enough to make me think I might have a problem.

We were working at the Big Powder Horn Ski Hill north of Bessemer putting in screw anchors one morning when but for the grace of God I should have been killed. These were ten-foot pieces of metal rod, and we used a digger truck to literally screw them into the ground. We had it halfway in when it stopped and wouldn't go any further. I told John, the guy on the truck, to back it out a ways and try again. It took about six times of doing that, but we ultimately got it to the proper depth. Then I unhooked the boom from the rod and stored the boom, and we drove away.

At around one thirty in the afternoon, our foreman showed up and asked if we had any trouble with the anchor that morning. We explained to him what had occurred and he stated no wonder because we had drilled the anchor through a sixteen thousand volt power cable, knocking out power to most of the ski hill. Neither the boss nor the power company could figure out how we were still alive. Go figure.

Another time I was riding in a digger truck going from Ironwood to Bessemer. One of the rear-dual tires on the side where the boom sat literally blew off the truck, passing us on the road as it went out into the woods. It took the driver all five lanes of highway to keep the truck from rolling. I remember yelling at him to hang on to it. When he was finally able to bring it to a stop, we must have sat there for a couple of minutes in our own thoughts. We were in the middle of the five-lane highway, and the truck was leaning heavy to the right, the moment it sunk in that we were still alive, we started to laugh. The release of stress comes in many ways.

It was also in Ironwood where I learned to use snow shoes. They gave me a pair of five-foot Alaskans and then used me for entertainment as they would knock me off them and laugh as I struggled to get back on. The snow that year was about eight feet deep, so it was a good time to learn. You had to varnish them every so often to keep the leather tight. We also cut pieces of truck inner tubes, attaching them to the snowshoe, making it easier to slip them on and off our boots. I remember watching a cable repairman working on an aerial cable while sitting on a seat box. He had to have been twenty feet in the air and was sitting on top of a snow drift. One morning I jumped into the car to warm it up, and there was nothing that moved on the car. It was totally frozen. The car started after a bit, but it took a long time to warm up enough to drive it. They said it was fifty below that morning, and I can believe it.

I was not at the top of my pay scale yet so money was real tight. There was one time when I had to take toilet paper from work so we would have some at the apartment. There was another instance when we had just enough money to make a big pot of goulash that we hoped would last the week. On Monday the boss told us to pack our bags because we were going out of town to work. While I was gone, Peg said the neighbor couple had her over for a few meals that week, and with that plus the goulash, she had enough to eat.

While in Ironwood, I was working on the road more than I was home. We always referred to the distance between towns by how many beers it took to get there. We drank from the time we left on Sunday night till we got back on Friday night. The majority of the material we took down in the winter was open wire along with the poles they were on. This is the wire you see in old pictures tied to cross arms, and there could be up to five arms on a pole. The majority of the wire was copper so it was important to get it back on cable reels and take it to be salvaged.

Once I was sitting on a snowmobile, not paying much attention to what was going on around me. I thought I was safe because I was a little ways from shore on the frozen Michigamme River. John and I had been taking turns cutting down old telephone poles and then leaving them where they fell. He yelled just in time, for when I looked up, the end of a cross arm was heading straight for my head. I wrapped myself around the cowling of the snow machine as the cross arm hit the seat, brushing the back of my jacket. Another time we got a two-track Bombardier snow machine stuck way back in the bush alongside the railroad tracks. We tried to yank it out with two other machines but couldn't budge it. We left it there for the night, and then the next morning we stopped a train going through and they pulled it out for us. Back then they would stop if you needed help out in the bush. I doubt a train would stop now.

We didn't know it, but the men in the line crews were a dying breed. We were the last of the old-style telephone company lineman. The new people being hired into the crews would never know what it was like to do line work the old-fashioned way. There would be no open wire, no placing lead cable or even building pole leads. If the new guys didn't have a bucket truck, they whined like puppies that had been taken away from their mother.

I loved climbing poles, even after I got out of the line crew, and used a ladder only when I had to. There was one time though in Hancock, Michigan, when I left the motel room in the morning wearing tennis shoes rather than lineman boots. I wonder if it had anything to do with the night before. The foreman didn't like me and wouldn't let me go back to my room and change into my boots. All day I climbed in tennis shoes, not giving the creep the satisfaction of seeing how bad I was hurting. At the end of the day I could hardly walk, vowing never to be that stupid again. Imagine someone with a drinking problem saying they are not going to do anything stupid again.

One winter we spent a great deal of time working in Iron River, Michigan so we got to know the locals extremely well. One morning I came to in John's room, and I was lying on the floor naked, wondering how I had managed to get there. He said he found me wandering the halls of the hotel, naked with a bottle of wine in my hand, when he came back from the bar. I couldn't remember anything about the night before, let alone why I would be wandering the halls naked.

I called the desk for someone to meet me at my room with a key. As I stood there in the hallway with one of John's towels wrapped around me, this guy kept giving me a polite smile as he unlocked my door. While I was walking to my room to meet him, I kept wondering where my clothes were. Was I ever glad to see them lying on the floor when I walked into the room; so this must have been my starting point.

Another time in the same town I got lost, going back to the hotel. There was an alley that ran straight from the hotel to a bar the next block over. You could sit in the window of the bar and see the front door of the hotel. On this particular night, I was heading back to the hotel. The guys recounted to me later that they sat watching while I staggered around that alley for an hour trying to find my way out. I would come back to this same town toward the end of my drinking career.

It was a ten-hour drive from Midland to Ironwood, with Peg wanting to get closer to her relatives so I called Telephone Joe, the head guy for the Upper Peninsula, to see if there were openings in Marquette. He told me there were and to put in for one and he would see that I got it. Joe was that kind of man in that he had come up through the ranks and believed in taking care of his people.

John and I were on the road at the time, working in Marinette, Michigan, just across the river from Menomonee, Wisconsin. We were staying at the usual style of motel that we stayed in with a bar and a restaurant just down the street. I met this woman about thirty-five years old at the bar, and she asked if I would ride back to her place so she could check on her kids. When we got there, for some reason the Bible came up, so we sat at her kitchen table drinking beer and reading from the Bible. After we left her place, she gave me a ride to my hotel, and when she was backing up, she backed into the wall of my room, cracking the plaster inside. She came in and we had a few more beers, and she left a couple of hours later. The owner of the motel was really ticked the next day when I told him I didn't know anything about it.

I finally got in touch with Telephone Joe, and he said to head for Wakefield, pack up our stuff, and report to Marquette the following Monday morning. I left for Wakefield that night. Peg and I packed up our belongings and headed to sunny Marquette. It didn't take long to pack the U-Haul truck because we really had nothing except for the appliances, a few couches, and some chairs.

We rented a house on a main street between Bunny Bread and the Ford dealer. Peg found work at the medical center in the billing department so she was able to stay busy and was making new friends. She seemed more content, and we were only an hour and a half from her family in McMillan. It was still a six-hour trip to Midland, but that was more manageable than the ten hours we use to have. I was still in the line crew so that meant out of town work, but now Peg had people to hang out with when I was gone.

The house we rented was heated with a coal furnace that had an automatic feeder connected to it. I had never been involved with a coal furnace before and didn't know a thing about them. I asked around at work, and some of the guys came over and filled me in on it. I would fill the feeder twice a day and then clean out the clinkers as needed. It took a while to realize what a true clinker looked like so I threw away a lot of good coal. Marquette was a college town and also had KI Sawyer Air Force base over by Gwinn. I don't think Marquette was really that big at the time, but when you added in the college and air base the number swelled, making it the largest town in the UP.

There were more young people working in Marquette at AT&T so we had a lot more people to do things with, which to me meant drinking. Peg got along well with my coworkers wives as we all drank and enjoyed getting together.

Even the guys who had kids would stop at Remilard's on the way home for a couple of beers. This was a downtown bar the power and telephone company linemen stopped in rather frequently. One of the power company's lead lineman was sitting at the bar one night when a guy he had words with the night before walked up to the window and fired a twelve-gauge shotgun at him. The lineman saw his attacker first and was able to get out of the line of fire before he assumed room temperature. I think there was something about someone getting hit in the head with a bottle about the same time. It could be a rather rowdy place at times, like most bars.

Bruce Sandstrom and I had volunteered to work on a Saturday when Peg's brother and girlfriend were coming to visit. We all had planned to go out that night when I got off work, but instead Bruce and I, after getting to the Bell garage, decided we didn't want to work that day and headed for the bar. We spent the better part of the day there, and by the time I got back to the house, I was drunk. Peg was as mad as a hornet when she saw the shape I was in, but drunk is drunk. They put me to bed and went out that night. It always came back to what I wanted and when I wanted it.

On another night a bunch of us left work, heading to the bar. After the bars closed, I went to a friend's apartment and stayed there drinking until the sun was coming up. When I got home, and the first thing I saw when I went in the door was the coffee pot percolating. If you want to dance, sooner or later you have to pay the fiddler, and that morning I paid the bill in full.

On this sunny spring day, three of us were working with two different trucks by Lake Superior in Harvey. The two guys in the other truck were from Escanaba, and both of them were good men. One had just hired in, and the other one had about as much time as I did. After the job was finished, we hung around the trucks talking a little and then headed for the Bell garage in Marquette. They were riding in an International line truck, and I had my digger truck.

As they made a ninety-degree turn crossing some railroad tracks, their truck slid sideways. They had hit some black ice, and when the rear duals hit the railroad tracks, it started a slow roll, going over on its side. I applied my brakes, almost sliding into them because it was so slippery. I saw the driver kicking the windshield out and screaming that the other guy was trapped under the truck. He had tried to jump as the truck was going over, and the truck landed on top of him. The truck was sitting on the railroad tracks with a curve about a quarter mile down the tracks. All I could think of was a train coming around that curve and taking the overturned truck and the guy pinned under it down the railroad tracks. I told the driver to go to a house close by and have them call for an ambulance and police.

I pulled around their truck, setting up the digger to lift the International off the man who was pinned underneath. I yelled at the driver as he came back that I was going to run down and put flags on the track in case a train came. By then the police had showed up, and they tried to lift the truck but couldn't get it far enough off the ground to get the guy out. Then a guy drove down alongside the tracks on a side road, telling me what was going on. He took the flags from me, and I went back to operate the digger truck.

I knew the digger would lift the other truck; it just had to be done in the right sequence. I got the winch as tight as I could and then started to extend the boom straight up. Slowly the truck came off him, with his head and then his upper body swinging free, but his legs were trapped under the pike poles, holding him to the truck. It took two guys to break them in half so we could get him out. He died a week later from massive injuries. I can still see him hanging upside down from the truck, with his body swinging back and forth. The driver said he yelled for him to stay inside the truck, but it was too late because he was already halfway out the door. I was told later that his wife had lost two previous husbands in car accidents and now this. We never know where life will take us or where it will end. I have often wondered over the years if we had got him out quicker if the ending might have been different.

Around this time Peg's brother, Larry, was getting married, and they asked us to be in the wedding. The girl he was marrying was a friend of Peg's from high school so it was everyone knows everyone type of wedding. On the day of the wedding, I had just put on my tux and was standing outside of Larry's house drinking a beer when a blond woman with two small kids came down the street. She and her husband were in school with Peggy, and we would see them once in a while at parties when we lived in Midland. As we talked, she mentioned that she lived just down the street and her husband was at work. She suggested that I walk with her to her place and she would put the kids down for a nap. She let it be known that she wanted more than to talk over old times. I told her I appreciated the invite but there just wasn't enough time before we had to leave.

We made the trip to Midland fairly regularly now that we lived closer. There was one couple we always stayed with rather than relatives because they liked to drink as much as I did and the relatives didn't. On one occasion we had been drinking most of the day and then went over to this other couple's house. There were three couples there, with everyone sitting on the floor rather than on furniture. I was out in the kitchen doing something, and when I went back to the living room, I saw Peg lying on the floor talking to the guy who owned the house. For some reason that didn't sit well with me, so I walked up drop kicking her in the back.

They threw me out of the house, and I don't remember anything until I woke up at three in the morning back at the other friend's house. Peg was awake and showed me this huge, ugly bruise on her back, wanting to know why I did it. How could I tell her why when I didn't know myself? As I said before, the insanity was always just below the surface and I never knew when or how to stop it when it reared its ugly head. All I could do was apologize and hope she would eventually forgive me.

The simplest answer to the question she asked would be one I heard years later, I did it because that is what alcoholics do. That does not excuse me from what I did, but it is what alcoholics and people with untreated PTSD do. It's a horrifying existence to live inside a body that screams at you every second you're not drunk or high. There are so many voices, and they come at you from all directions. Did I wish I had not done the things I did? You bet, but life is what it is, and there was nothing at the time I could do to change it.

We left the next morning for Marquette. She had a bruised back, and I, as usual, had a hangover. After some time in Marquette, it was decided we would build a house and while doing so became friends with the builders. They liked to party on the weekends so it gave Peg someone else to hang out with during the week when I was on the road. They were a nice couple but would eventually get divorced like almost everyone else we knew. We also had friends who lived in the neighborhood we were building in. Peg was trying to make the marriage work so we went to counseling; with this psychologist telling us there was no way we would ever get a divorce. That answer made you feel all good and warm inside, but I wasn't betting any money on the outcome. Later I heard the guy liked his weed a little more than he should have.

By now I was working on a bucket truck that allowed you to carry both strand and cable reels, lashing them together as they came off the truck going to the pole. Over a period of time, I became very productive using this truck. It took two men to work the truck, and we were sent all over the Upper Peninsula working jobs. There was only one other truck like it north of the Mackinaw Bridge so we were in demand.

Sonny Guizzetti and I were working in Escanaba when John Niemi, the foreman at the time, told us we would not be going back to Marquette as we had been told. In response I drop-kicked a wastebasket across his office, telling him what he and the company could do. At the end of my tirade, he starts to laugh, telling us we were still going to Iron Mountain instead of Marquette. It just never ended.

When I finally made it back to Marquette, there wasn't much left of the marriage. After I had been home a short time, I took a day of vacation while Peg went to work. I had planned to go to the local store and buy a twelve pack of beer and a gallon of wine. When Peg got home that afternoon, I was sitting in the middle of the garage floor with the gallon of wine between my legs. She told me later in life that was the moment when she lost all respect for me. I think it was a few days later we were talking and she asked what I wanted out of the marriage, and I said a divorce.

How do drunks know what they want? Most of the time a drunk can't even think straight. A divorce seemed like the easier way, so I filed, and six months later it was over! Between the time of separation and divorce I would sometimes go to her apartment in town, and we always got into an argument. One time it ended with me slapping her around, and I realized I had to stay totally away from her. She wanted the tax returns for that year, which was pretty much what we had in equity on the house. After the judge granted the divorce, we went across the street to a bar, and I bought her a beer. She should have had more than a violent, abusive drunk for a husband. An alcoholic does not ruin people's lives; we destroy them. It can also be said that we don't have relationships; we take prisoners.

Chapter 20

Mom started drinking again sometime in 1974. They sold their mobile home, and she and Duane moved to a very rough section of Saginaw. They picked up right where they had left off because that is what alcoholism does. It continues in your body as if you had never stopped. Over the next several years, the nice life they had before turned into nothing more than an existence. Grandma Brewster had moved in with them while they weren't drinking but lived a hard life after they started until she moved in with Aunt Lola and Uncle John. Grandma called me a few times to ask if I would move back and maybe Mom would slow down on her drinking. I couldn't help myself; how was I going to help Mom? I was hung over on the day of Grandma Brewster's funeral, with my cousin Ralph Cady nudging me awake so I could carry the coffin because I was a pall bearer. That was not the proper way to honor her memory. She would have been very ashamed of me if she knew the shape I was in that day.

Dad and Barb had Joe and Chris together, but there were also two older daughters from Barb's previous marriage. It appeared to Carol, Butch, and me that Dad and Barb really didn't want us around. We thought that because of their actions toward us. When I would come back to Midland, we all got together at least once, but more and more Dad placed his new family first and we went on the back burner. I really didn't care because I never lived near them and only came back to Midland maybe twice a year after the divorce. But I know it bothered Carol and Butch.

I never expected anything from Dad or Mom, so it was what it was. For that matter, I didn't expect anything from anybody except to be left alone. I felt that Barb thought if we were around too much it would draw Dad's attention away from her family, and she didn't want that. I never really liked being around them because they enjoyed manipulating their kids, and if there wasn't chaos going on in their lives, they would create it. They complained about what was going on around them but at the same time thrived on it. One time Butch and I were at Dad's house when Joe screwed up the chain on his bike. The first thing the old man did was smack him on the back of the head, calling him a few names. I told him if I ever saw him smack Joe again he could expect the same from me. He looked up as if he was going to say something but then thought better of it.

Dad hadn't drunk for about fifteen years at the time, but he never fixed the problem, which was his thinking. I think the older he got, the meaner and ornerier he became. He always believed his sister purposely didn't contact the Red Cross until after his brother was buried so he would not make it home for the funeral. Between her and Grandma Spencer, that man carried around a lot of pain and resentments until the very end. I talked to him close to his death, telling him to let go of the resentments because all those people were dead. He had outlived them all. He said he hated them more now than when the situation happened, and if he could, he would dig up the bodies and smacked them just for the sake of smacking them. I know he gave his second family a lot more material things than he did his first one, but that was OK because the three of us learned how to survive by living through what we did.

Do I believe Dad and Mom loved us? It might not make sense to some people, but I believe they did. In the very beginning I think they loved us as much as any parent could love their child. But as life evolved and the alcohol took over, their love started to melt away as winter snow must give way to a day of sunshine. They were caught up in their own demons and had no defense to resist the excitement of self-indulgence. If you don't fix the main cause of the problem then it stays with you for the rest of your life. I believe they wanted to love us and during some intervals were able to.

I wasn't close to my family because I hadn't been around them for any length of time since I was seventeen years old. I didn't trust people or even like them much. I drank to deaden the pain and rage inside of me even though at the time I didn't realize that was what I was doing. I would spend the rest of my life wanting to stop the train as it went through town, get on it, and go to the end of the line. But the only problem with that was I would be there when it arrived.

After the divorce, in my own sick way I thought I was footloose and fancy free, not realizing that the cords of bondage to alcohol were to intensify in ways I couldn't imagine. I would get sores in my mouth from the amount of alcohol I was drinking and would have to stop until they healed. When this happened, I smoked dope to numb my reality. I didn't have the patience to roll little punk joints but made them as big as my thumb.

You have to remember I was after effect, not enjoyment. When I wasn't working on the road, I would drink at home rather than go to bars. I was a loner and was becoming a recluse, which made for a rather small circle of people I associated with. I spent a lot of time on the road over the next couple of years because I was single, and why not?

One time I was in Houghton-Hancock, Michigan when I went to a Chinese restaurant at about ten thirty at night after having sat in the bar since four o'clock. I spent about an hour and a half in there eating and drinking, and when I came out the front door, I had no idea where I was or even what country I was in. I backed up against the wall, staring down the street each way. I knew I wasn't in Vietnam because I didn't have my rifle and I wasn't in Korea because the smell wasn't right. Maybe it was Thailand or Japan—who knew? I broke into a cold sweat and started to shake. Slowly it came back to me where I was, but that would not be the last time this happened.

Toward the end of my time in the line crews, the company put me on the road by myself. I was antisocial, which made it hard to keep a partner. I went through partners like people changed their socks, but I still put out a lot of productivity with the truck. When I wore out my welcome in one town, they would ship me to another, and on and on it went.

Peg had hooked up with one of the cable technicians, and for some reason I didn't like that and made their lives miserable whenever I could. You had to remember that I was in charge of the world and decided what was going to happen in it. Later more than one person told me that the construction and installation departments were continuously wondering when I was going to come through the door with my gun. The guy Peg was seeing must have walked in every morning wondering if this was going to be the day I decided to take him out. I think that might have been one of the reasons they kept me on the road. I remember him hitting me once, and it infuriated me so much I grabbed him and shook him like a rag doll. The punch didn't hurt; it was the principle of it, whatever that principle meant to a person in my state of mind.

They shipped me back to Iron River, only this time we went as a full crew with guys from all over the Upper Peninsula. Most of them were from Sault St. Marie, and those guys were just plain nuts. There was a strip club in town we went to once in a while, and I would always pull my chair right up to the circle they danced in. There was no stage for them to dance on so it was on the floor. I would see the girls who danced there at the bar in the hotel where we all stayed. After about a week of this, one of them asked if I wanted to go upstairs for some fun before she went to work. They weren't prostitutes so it was just for something to do. She was about twenty-three years old. She was a very pretty girl with a great body and must have thought I was nuts when I told her no. I was three sheets to the wind and did not want to stop drinking just for a roll in the sack. I was at the stage of alcoholism where drinking came first over everything, including a romp in the bedroom.

Ken, who came from New Mexico originally but lived and worked out of Sault St. Marie, and I hit it off, with a lot of drinking and carousing. Eventually he hooked up with some woman from Iron River, married her, and moved back to New Mexico. That's way too far to go look for a wife if you ask me. He went to a bar one night by himself and got in a fight with one of the locals. He told me later that as they were pulling him off the guy, he grabbed the guy's hair, and when he got him to the right point, he kicked the guy in the head. When his head hit the floor, his eyes crossed. From what I heard, it took the doctors awhile to get them back to normal.

This was the same bar that one of our guys was beat on in the men's bathroom. Two brothers followed him in, and after working him over, they kicked his head into a cast-iron heater. When they found him lying there, the police were called, and an ambulance took him to the hospital. He had a concussion and was pretty bruised up.

About a week later, I was sitting at the same bar by myself, staring into the back mirror like most drunks do. Usually no one sat next to me unless they knew me so I was pretty much left alone. I ask the barmaid, who had become a friend, if there is such a thing in a bar, why none of the locals ever tried taking me out like they did my buddy. She shook her head, telling me to take a good long look into the mirror at what people saw when they came through the front door.

I looked, and what I saw shocked me. The animal that was looking back was not someone I knew. He had shoulder-length hair and a full scraggly beard that was unkempt; with his hair looking like it hadn't seen a comb in a month. There was no expression on his face, and he weighed around 230 pounds. But the scary part was his eyes; there was no sign of life in them, only a vacant stare. A few minutes later, the barmaid wanted to know if I liked what I saw. I told her no, and she said that was the reason people left me alone. I was twenty-six at the time but looked ten years older. I was almost at the end of my road but still had a few more miles to go. The foreman who was in charge of the crew while we were there eventually retired in Iron River, marrying a local women. They bought a bar in the area and settled down, but it must not have gone well for I heard later that he killed himself.

I was working in Sault St. Marie when the *Edmond Fitzgerald* went down on Lake Superior. When I walked out of the bar at around 11:30 that night, you could not see across the sidewalk because the snow was coming down so hard, with the wind blowing it sideways. It was one of the worst storms I had seen while living in the Upper Peninsula. I spent most of that winter in the Sault, and it was one of the coldest on record. There were places we could not get the truck in so we had to climb the poles, but the problem was the ice storms that came off Lake Superior. We would use a hatchet to beat the ice from the poles, climb for a ways, and then beat more ice off. Sometimes the ice would be an inch thick or more on the poles and lines. It was a dangerous winter for being a lineman because you never knew when power lines were going to come down on you or a sheet of ice would fall from above as you climbed the pole, taking you with it.

One morning we went for breakfast after leaving the Bell garage so I could get something in my stomach and settle the jitters from the night before. As my partner and I were sitting there, I heard people talking in the booth in back of us. He was telling them about this crazy bearded guy who was on his hands and knees in the Michigan Bell garage that morning. He said the guy was breaking ice around the floor drains and then splashing the water on his face, trying to cool himself off. He told them it was funny to watch but the guy really needed to get help before he died. Finally, honesty from someone even though he didn't know he was giving it.

I passed out in my motel room one night at about eight thirty, waking up again a little after midnight. I couldn't get back to sleep so I walked next door to the bar, ordering five triple shots. I downed one after another and then went back to my room, passing out again.

Whatever my body experienced and found enjoyable it wanted more of. It didn't matter whether it was booze, women, pornography, drugs, violence, or chaos; I was captivated by them all. I actually hated violence but at the same time was drawn to it like a moth to a flame. I was in bondage to everything that was killing me and didn't care. There are people who will not comprehend that, but the statement is not meant for you but for the ones who do identify with it. There are Christians who would say if I had only said the right prayer with enough faith all the things that were killing me would go away. That is very religious and pious sounding, but that is not the way life works for people like me. It is a long, hard process, and most people die on the journey.

In July of 1975, I wrote some things down. I have no idea why I did it because I was not someone who wrote, and in my state of mind, I could only comprehend them later.

July 21, 1975
In the rivers and valleys of heaven the sun shone on,
And the thing that was is still but you
as a human have to seek it.

Only a person's heart is true their actions
are of another time and place
Time is heavenly and heaven is time at its utmost
And then there was me!

July 21, 1975
I wish that I might be as much as I hoped to be.
Darkness is as one that is there beholds it.

July 24, 1975
The clouds broke and the sun was
there and the sun was there
But who made the sun?
God made the sun and the heavens.
The one who does not understand this is one
who does not understand the moment.

July 24, 1975
And then there was me!

I recognize now there was someone inside of me crying to get out, but it was not to be at this time.

I would go back to Marquette on the weekends from Sault St. Marie and would sometimes pass Peg and the cable technician heading the other way. It always amazed me that they got shocked looks on their faces when they recognized it was me. I have wondered if they thought I was going to spin the car around and follow them. The anger had pretty much subsided, but then I heard he was beating her. Imagine that—she found someone just like me. What I didn't expect was my reaction to it. It pissed me off, with some words passing between us. He thought he was bad, but at the same time he knew I was way crazier than him. It's amazing how that affects someone. I don't know if he ever did it again, but if he did, I never found out. It was okay for me to do it in a drunken stupor but not him. Now that's insane.

I didn't go back to Marquette that often because we worked most Saturdays, but every time I did I'd stop at the McMillan bar. Usually I would bump into Peg's aunt or uncle there and have a few beers with them. One time when I was leaving for some reason I leaned over and French kissed her aunt good-bye. That was one shocked aunt as I walked out the door. I saw her at the Marquette hospital a number of years later, and she eventually died from a heart attack at a young age. She asked me at that time why I had quit drinking. I told her it was because I couldn't stop. Like I said, they were nice people, and I enjoyed their company.

I can't remember exactly when I transferred out of the line crew, but I do know why. We went out to hang some cable and down guys, but as I pulled the down guy tight, the rod came out of the ground. Another crew had put them in, and most of them pulled out as we tried to tension them up. After we dug them up to see what the problem was, we found the crew had not tightened the bolt on the bottom.

Even in my state of mind, I knew it was time to get into another department. There were some openings in the installation department, so I went there. You had to go into customer homes, installing dial tone and the phones that went with it, so it was back to school for me with a lot of on-the-job training. There was a lot of traveling back and forth to Grand Rapids, Michigan, because that was where the main school for Michigan Bell was located.

I side-swiped a car while there as I tried to turn a corner, and yes, I was drunk. It was an older car with a young couple driving. We pulled into a gas station, and they accepted three hundred dollars because it was close to Christmas and they needed the money. They were glad to get the cash, and I was glad not to go to jail for drunk driving. My cousin Karen Phillips lived in Shields, and I always stopped at her place on the way down and back. She has a special place in my heart, and I enjoyed the times we spent together.

There was a woman we nicknamed Bear Cub because she looked like a little bear cub going up a tree when she climbed a pole. She had moved up from Ohio, and our paths would keep crossing even to this day. Her name is Sue Bowers, but everyone at Bell referred to her as Bear Cub. She says I was the one who nicknamed her, but I believe it was someone else. She would tell you in no uncertain terms what she thought and took no crap from anyone. I still consider her a friend even though we don't see each other much and only talk about once a year. She could tell others what they didn't want to hear but at the same time let them know she was not judging them. That's a remarkable quality if you can do it.

Sue told me that she heard about this insane lineman shortly after she arrived, and everything she heard made her believe it would be best if she never met the guy. She said the first time she saw me was when I drove past in the bucket truck, and I looked like someone who belonged in a padded cell. I want to say the first time she called me a big marshmallow like to put me over the cliff.

My life in the installation department was as different as night and day when compared to the line crew. The installation crew was actually close because they never went on the road except in extreme emergencies. At the time there was an installation crew and a separate repair crew. In the end they were all combined, with everyone doing both jobs. For some reason I got along fairly well with the installation side even though I continued to drink.

We were at a company party one night at the American Legion Hall in Marquette when Pete grabbed me, and over the tables we went. I found out later he thought I had said something I hadn't. He had me by the throat while I was hitting him in the head with a wooden salt shaker. I am certain it had nothing to do with the amount of beer we had consumed. There must have been seven or eight guys who piled on. I think Bear Cub even got involved. The following Monday morning I was walking down a hallway at work when we saw each other. Both of us started to laugh at the same time as we went to the break room to get a cup of coffee.

All in all I got along fairly well with the new crew, and if they didn't like me, they at least put up with me. Carol, another women in the crew, and I started to see each other, but there were no emotional attachments because neither of us wanted one. She had just come out of a bad divorce and didn't want to get emotionally involved with anyone. I believe it was less than six months from the time we started seeing one another until it came to an end.

Just before we stopped seeing one another, Carol had a dinner party at my house for my twenty-ninth birthday where she gave me the best present I had ever received: nine fifths of different brands of hard liquor. I remember the party starting and sitting at a table but nothing else. The next morning I came to on the living room floor, naked with two empty bottles of booze lying next to me. Carol was nowhere to be found, and when I called her later, she wouldn't talk about what had happened. To this day I don't know what took place that night, but it was the end of us seeing each other outside of work. This happened on March 3, 1976, and for the next seventeen days, my life would be a living nightmare.

On the way home from work, I always stopped at the M-28 Market for my nightly supply of alcohol. It was usually a case of beer and bottle of wine or else three bottles of wine with a twelve pack. I did this every night, passing out by ten or eleven o'clock. Sometimes I would make it to bed, but I usually passed out on the couch or floor and would come to in the morning with the television still going. I could not handle the silence so I would keep something on for the noise. Toward the end of my drinking, I'd call people late at night just to argue with them while calling them every vulgar name I could think of. I was mean and vindictive while drinking, and this was one small way of payback. As usual, the ones you target are the ones closest to you. It was mostly family, and by the end they wanted nothing to do with me. If they heard my voice on the phone, they hung up.

Some nights I didn't drink enough to pass out, and I'd stagger to the bedroom. I always had a bottle on the nightstand and my 9mm pistol under the pillow with a round in the chamber. There were nights when I'd come instantly awake so terrified I couldn't move, with the whole bed wet from night sweats. I would be so overtaken by panic and fear that all I could move were my eyes. I'd lay there, my mind screaming at me to move, that they were in the house and would be coming through the door and

I needed my gun. The sheer terror of these nights was overwhelming.

Daylight gave me some reprieve from the horror of the night, and work kept my mind from hearing all the voices arguing in my head. I never went down state anymore, and I didn't leave the house when I got home from work. I remember the phone ringing once, and it was the neighbor across the street telling me to either pull the curtains shut or put some clothes on. He thought it was funny, but these were the things that made me comprehend how far down the ladder of life I had fallen.

My trashcans were full of whiskey, beer, wine bottles, and little else. I was ashamed to show myself outside the house and didn't like mirrors because I hated the image that glared back at me. I was drinking to live and living to drink. I put on a show at work, but from the time I left work until I went back the next morning, it was totally irrational and terrifying in my world. I was bound so tightly I was suffocating. My nerves were shot, and I wasn't eating.

There was no reliability in my thought process, and my mind went wherever it wanted to. I knew I was going crazy, but at no time did I think it was the alcohol that was responsible for my problems. How could it be? It was my lover, confidant, and protector. It allowed me to sleep at night and kept reality at bay. All I could think about was how I had been wronged—by who I didn't know just that I had been. I still had a few bottles of booze Carol had given me for my birthday so I finished them off. During the previous year, I never woke up with a hangover because I never sobered up and would have blown over a .20 at any given time.

It was during this seventeen-day period that *Readers Digest* came out with a story about this man who had a drinking problem but was able to put his life back together. I remember sitting there reading the story over and over while drinking my nightly supply. There was also a program on the local television station about a married couple from Marquette that was able to quit drinking and stop the insanity in their lives. I also watched this program while drinking, wondering what they looked like because their faces were blacked out. It was a lot to think about and I was glad it worked for them, but alcohol was not my problem. My problem was the world didn't understand or appreciate me.

This thought process continued into the last week of my drinking. I started on Friday after getting off work, but as much as I drank, I could not get drunk to the level I needed to be at. For an alcoholic, that is not a good thing. I drank to escape reality, and not being allowed to do so was more than I was prepared to go through.

On Saturday afternoon, I was sitting on the couch wondering what was happening to me. My friend John Barley Corn had always worked, but now he was letting me down. I had a bottle of booze and my 9mm pistol, and one of them was going to take care of the situation I found myself in. They were both there in front of me, and each time I stretched my arm toward the coffee table, I never knew which one I was going to pick up and put in my mouth. I didn't have outward shakes, but my insides were literally crawling. My nerves were fried, and my rational thinking was gone. The light had gone out at the end of the tunnel, and I did not believe it was ever coming back on. I would make them pay for doing this to me.

They would be sorry. Who they were I had no clue. It is appalling to realize that you have no future and your life is lacking meaning or purpose.

I drank most of the fifth of whiskey but still was no closer to escaping. The story I read in *Reader's Digest* and the television show about the married couple came to me. In both the story and television show they referred to God, but I blamed him for what had happened to me. How many times had I prayed for help when I was a kid with no answer coming? He didn't care about me or he wouldn't have stood off to the side watching as I went through what I did. Didn't I say the prayer that Billy Graham told me to with my first wife? Life didn't get better after that; it got worse. Then during a moment of clarity, I knew no matter how this thing went, I couldn't go any further. With tears running down my face, I cried to whatever God was out there to either help me or kill me. I didn't care which. The only thing I wanted was for the pain to stop. I had lived with it for far too long. It had destroyed me, and it was never going to get better as long as I relied on myself.

Just then Kathy, an old drinking friend from the past, came to mind. I had not seen or talked to her for well over a year and was surprised when her name came to me. I knew I had to talk to her right away but didn't know why. She lived in Marquette so I called, hoping she would answer, not knowing what I would do if she didn't. After a couple of rings she picked up, and I started to describe what was going on with me. She stopped me, saying to pick up a can of coffee and come over. This was at about six o'clock in the evening, and I wouldn't leave her place until well after midnight.

When I got there, Kathy put on a pot of coffee, and we sat down at her kitchen table, where she began to tell me what had taken place in her life. She hadn't had a drink for seven months, saying she met regularly with a group of people who were trying to do the same. They told her she had to stop picking it up and clean up the wreckage from her past. She said it wasn't easy but her life had become more bearable. Kathy always was a beautiful woman, but there was gentleness about her now that I had never seen before. She told me the people she met with were going to get together the following night, and I should consider coming with her.

From this point forward every time I write "meeting," it will be referring to a gathering of people who are trying to stay sober and clean up their lives. I said I would pick her up the following night and headed for home. She had given me a lot to think about.

Chapter 21

On March 21, 1976, I picked up Kathy, and we headed to my first meeting. The beginning of my journey would take place in Marquette at a house on High Street; it's a parking lot now. As we went up the sidewalk, Kathy turned and asked me if I was scared. I told her no I wasn't scared; I was terrified. That was the first bit of honesty that had come out of my mouth in a really long time. I knew deep in my soul that if this didn't work, I had no place else to go. I would either die or be committed to an institution of some kind. I had no idea what to expect when I walked in that door; after all, there were alcoholics in there.

As Kathy opened the door, I took a deep breath and stepped into an unknown future. It seemed like everyone knew Kathy, and she introduced me around, telling me to sit next to an older bald-headed man. There were two guys about my age who seemed to be in charge, and they were talking and laughing about stuff that just days before I had been thinking of blowing my brains out for. There were maybe twenty people there of all ages, and each of them had a say about how they got there.

When it came my turn, the old guy beside me glanced my way, nodding as if to say it was okay for me to talk. I told them who I was—that my life was a cesspool and

I couldn't stop drinking. It seemed as if they understood because most of them nodded in agreement, with several of them coming over after the meeting to give me their phone numbers, telling me it would work out if I didn't pick up a drink and to come back tomorrow night. I left that meeting with a ray of hope that hadn't been there when I went in.

We went back to Kathy's, and I spent another couple of hours talking with her before I went home. As I drove home that night on Highway 28, the moon was positioned over the lake, looking as if I could drive right into it. I took that as a good omen. I went to bed as soon as I got home, falling immediately asleep and slept the whole night through. That was the first time I had done that in years. To actually fall asleep and then wake up was euphoric to me.

When I woke up, I couldn't wait to get to the meeting that night. I liked that little ray of hope I had gotten there the night before and wanted more of it. I told people at work what I had done, with some saying they were glad and some laughing about it. One of the guys in the line crew wanted to bet me five hundred dollars that I wouldn't last a week, which I didn't accept.

Someone who has never struggled with an addiction will say you just stop and that's it. But I didn't know if I was going to stay dry for the next five minutes, let alone a week. I knew there was something at those meetings because I saw it in the faces of the people. I figured if I kept going that sooner or later I might obtain a little bit of it—that just maybe some of whatever they had might rub off on me. The people I met at the meetings took me under their care, giving me the encouragement and advice to make it through the day. They loved me when I couldn't love myself.

Don, the old guy Kathy sat me next to on the first night, told me not to try to understand anything right now but to just keep coming back. He played a pivotal role in my life for a while because he was one who steered me through the first months. He told me things I would have hit other people for saying, but I could not deny the things he was telling me were true. He was a major in the marine's during the Korean War. There were times when I believed he thought he was still in the corp.

I found out later that he was the same age as my dad. His wife, Joan, was a wonderful person in the way she treated and cared for people. She would often tell me she loved me, with me responding for her to stick it. I was amazed at how gracious she was, and I never heard anyone say anything critical of her. She gave me a blank book and told me to write down my thoughts as I traveled along the road of sobriety. I did that for about five years and then stopped for a while, continuing later in life.

About one and half years after I met Joan, she got cancer. Again, I could not understand why she would be taken while others who deserved to die were left. Just before she passed I told her how much she meant to me and how much I loved her. She told me that she had always known that. She fought the cancer long and hard but it finally won out. The legacy that she left stills lives on in the lives of people she helped and the testimony of her dying sober.

A short time after I started going to meetings I met the married couple that was on television. His name was Dick and I frequently stopped to talk over things that were bothering me at his place of employment. He kept me from doing some real stupid things during the time I was around him. Both he and his wife were people that cared deeply about those still suffering from John Barleycorn. She was not only an alcohol counselor but took a lot of women under her care outside of her job. They gave freely of themselves and I never saw them allow personality conflicts to interfere with helping anyone.

The people I met when I first came to meetings were very influential to my staying sober and the beginning of a change in my life. They never gave up on me even when there were times I wanted to give up on myself. I would go to meetings, and each time there was something new I would learn about myself and how to deal with life on life's terms. That doesn't mean I liked what they were telling me all the time, but it does mean I would take it home and think about it.

When I had been around for a few weeks, I was told I could start washing ashtrays and wiping down the tables. I thought it was an honor that they trusted me to do that, and I wasn't about to let them down. It was a good reason to come early and stay late. Anyone who had a little sober time I placed next to God, and sad to say, I had them on a pedestal. That would change as some went back out and others drifted away, never to return.

The two guys I saw at my first meeting would become close friends of mine, teaching me a lot about staying sober. One of them was Jim, and he was a character who liked to ride his Harley Davidson. He told me he had taken his mother out for dinner just after getting sober. As the meal progressed, some fruit was brought to the table, and as soon as he put it in his mouth, he tasted booze. He said without even thinking he spit it out, hitting his mother between the eyes. They had a good laugh about it, but it made him more aware of his surroundings when it came to alcohol. The first thing he did every morning was to make his bed and brush his teeth. I asked him why that was so important to him. His answer was that he didn't do it when he drank, and this was a way of putting good habits back in his life. It made sense to me, so I tried to find things I could do that would put structure in my own life.

I would like to say all this was easy, but it was anything but. There were times I wanted to drink so bad that I could literally taste it. I had a calico cat named TJ, and she kept me from drinking on more than one occasion when I wanted to go back to the bottle. One time I came home from a meeting and around ten o'clock at night I wanted a drink so badly my whole body was shaking. I tried to call people, but no one answered. I also knew I wouldn't make it into town to look someone up because there were too many bars between me and town. I headed out the door and started to walk back and forth on the road in front of my house, talking to God. Looking down, I saw that TJ had come with me and walked by my side for the next hour or so. The moment the craving to drink left me so did TJ as she seemed to know that everything was okay.

I found a God after I came to the meetings, and it was the God I had always heard about. It was the God of the Bible and his Son, Jesus Christ, but it was not about religion this time but about a personnel relationship with him. Once the alcohol cleared from my brain, I knew he loved and cared for me because I was still alive, and looking back over my life, I could see where he had been directly involved even when I didn't think so. How else could everything have happened in the right sequence as far as the book, television show, and Kathy being brought to mind? God is always busy in my life; it is just that sometimes I only see him after the fact. Around this time I wrote the following:

July 8, 1976

To think that you are alone in the world is really one of the stupidest things you can do to yourself because you are never alone as long as there is God. And God is forever so you will never be alone. He is in us all. The one thing we have to do is look for him, and when we find him, we must love and cherish him as much as he does us. There is nothing he will not do for us if we pray and ask that his will be done in our lives. To be at peace with yourself is the most wonderful thing that can happen to anyone, but the only way you can attain that is to be at peace with God. There is so much I would like to say, but it is something inside of me, and I don't know how to put it in words. I only wish I could share it with someone, but there is no one to share it with. God knows what I'm saying, but it sure would be nice if someone here on earth would know it too. I guess that someday there will be someone, but it might be a long time in the future or it could be tomorrow. But I know it will happen someday.

It was a fascinating time for me because it seemed as if I was being born over and everything was new and fresh.

To watch a sunrise or a hummingbird drink the nectar of a flower was as if I was standing before God himself. In wonderment I beheld the miracle of life and wondered how I had missed it by such a great distance.

I was introduced to a person who would be a great influence on me both at the meetings and with my spiritual walk with God. His name was Vaughn, and I met him at an alcohol treatment center in Marquette. He was a counselor, and even though I didn't go to treatment, I would drop in at the center and talk to anybody who would listen. The staff allowed outside people to come in and talk to the patients, and in doing so we also were helped.

I had heard about Vaughn for some time and actually wanted to stay away from him because what I heard about him scared me. I imagined this big, rough, tough guy who chewed nails and beat little puppies. What I met was a soft-spoken individual who loved people but at the same time would not allow people to con him.

They had meetings at the hospital, and they were good to go to because they were a reminder of what I had been like just a few short months before. Some of the people I met there had gone through a lot more than I had. One guy would always end up living in roadside outhouses after he was kicked out of his house. He could stay sober for a time, and then off he would go again. I remember the time we literally dragged him down the hallway of the unit when the cops brought him in. Eventually he did get sober, staying that way until the day he died.

There was also Jack, who owned a grocery store and also had a camp on a lake down the road from me. His wife divorced him, and he would take off to the lake, leaving the store to be run by his help. We would go down there about every three months, hauling him out in an ambulance. He also finally got sober. There were a lot of success stories, but there were also sad ones. I worked with a man at Michigan Bell who helped me stay sober, but he went back to drinking. He walked in the front door of his house, picked up a twelve-gauge shotgun, walked out the back door, placed the barrel to his throat, and pulled the trigger. When I went to the funeral, I kept thinking it didn't have to end this way.

We had softball games and cook outs and would sit on the front porch of the meeting place talking the night away. I had become intertwined with a group of people who not only kept me alive but also gave me hope for the future. It was surprising to know there was still some worth in me.

Kathy introduced me to Ken, a guy she was seeing at the time, and we became good friends. Anytime there was something doing at the meeting place, all of us who came in about the same time would go together. Ken was well liked, and people seemed to congregate wherever he was. He eventually owned a restaurant, and I went there every morning to drink coffee and talk with whoever was there before going to work. Ken went on to get his teaching license and then a PhD in psychology. The last I heard he was somewhere in Massachusetts and still sober.

The mother of a guy I worked with was a cook there and adopted everyone who came in. She must have made an impression on me because after all this time I still think of her fondly. We watched out for each other and also confronted one another when it was needed. It was tough love before the smart people ever heard of the word. I remember Don kicking my butt every time he thought I needed it, and that seemed to be every time I saw him.

It was during this first year that I started to grow spiritually toward God. I was always asking people how I could be sure I had found the right God. The older people at the meetings would tell me to be patient and God would reveal himself to me more and more as I went along. Buy older I mean people who had been there for some time, not necessarily someone older in age.

One night I went home from a meeting, and while I was sitting at the kitchen table praying, God showed up. There was total love and peace that filled my very being. I looked up, and the whole room was filled with a golden glow that was everywhere. There were no shadows, just the warmth of the glow overpowering me with God's love. I don't know how long God stayed, but eventually the glow slowly faded.

It was a constant life of prayer for me in the beginning, for the only thing I sought was God's will for my life. When I was at work, my partner in the truck only heard me asking God to help me accept the things I could not change over the intercom. That was the most important prayer for me because there was nothing I could change. Prayer to me is having a conversation with God. Some people like their ritualistic prayers, but I find when I speak from my heart, God responds in kind.

There was one time when I was at my house in prayer after a meeting. I was on my knees in front of the couch when my spirit was given a view of mankind as it truly is. It was as if I was seeing the world with all of its inhabitants as God sees us, and it was heartbreaking. The depth of hurt, pain, loneliness, and every other emotion we experience was more that I could bear. I also saw the depravity of mankind against one another and how it brings heartbreak to God. I started to sob as I could sense the deepness of God's love toward us. As my body was racked by convulsions and the tears flowed like a river, I cried out for God to intervene. It seemed as if I spent a long time watching this unfold before me, and then it started to change. I saw Jesus at work with the Spirit of God changing lives while mediating for his people. Now I was not crying out of remorse but out of joy. From start to finish it took well over an hour, and the couch pillows were soaked by my tears.

Here are some things I wrote during this time period:

1976-1977

1

A soft, gentle touch or tender glance of compassion melts the hard, cold feelings of anger.

2

I feel torn tonight between what is.
The softness of a rose petal or the coldness of steel, the why and why not of it all!
What is right, and what is wrong?
Raging anger at his will or the acceptance of it in spite of myself! Who can say?
The great expectation of what I know is to come and the fear that it might not get here in time.

3

The pinks, yellows, reds, and gold's of a morning sunrise coming over the lake! The wonder at how anything so magnificent and beautiful can be so calming and serene. It takes something as simple as this to make me realize the promise that was told long ago. The simplicity of life depends on the actions of the people living it. They can either have a life of pain, hurt, and sadness or take things as they come, putting their faith in God. He is leaving the choice to us.

4

As the sun lifts its brilliant cap where the sky and sea meet as one, the moment is awakened with new life and hope.
Do I take the instant to meditate, or do I turn my head and look into the darkness, which is not yet fully gone?
Do I thank God for the time of peace, or do I curse the world for its darkness?
I take the time to let the moment encompass me with its love and compassion
And may I be willing to share with those who touch my life.

5

To love with a joy of complete giving, asking not and wanting not!
Toward this goal I walk.
With fear of rejection and doubt as to the ability to give!

The ever-changing inner being!
The anger at the inability to say, "I love you."
The soul crying out with a heart of stone in the cold, dark water of fear!

6

Think of that which is and not what you want it to be.
The thought of the moment is as an eternity to a lifetime.
For in that moment is all the knowledge of the universe.
Pray for wisdom and God's will for the moment and the joy of life is yours.

7

At times I think I will never have a person to share my life with, and it makes me sad. And there are times when I know I'm not ready to share with anyone. Or is it that I'm afraid to because in order to share, I would have to trust? And what if I do? The thought is there that they would eventually reject me. That they would take my emotions and toy with them as a cat does a mouse. That they would use me until I had nothing left to give and then discard me like an old newspaper. But where does the fear come from? Is faith not the opposite of fear? Faith in God that he will make things right . . . I think that for me it has to do with self. I get so wrapped up in self that I won't take the chance to _____?

I met Judy in the summer of 1976 when she moved up from South Carolina to be closer to her brother, who was a priest in the Upper Peninsula. She had four small children and was recently divorced. Judy had a southern drawl that could melt butter. She helped me to look at things from a woman's point of view and was not afraid to tell me when I was screwing up.

Judy went to college, getting a degree in nursing, and would retire from that career after thirty-five years. She told me I helped her pass her final exams, but I don't remember it. She said after a meeting we went back to her house for coffee, where she alluded to having problems studying for a final exam the next day. She said if she didn't pass this exam, she would have to take the course over, and that would cost her money she didn't have. She said I somehow simplified the way to study the book she was to take the exam on. Whether I did or not is irrelevant because she did pass the exam and had a very successful career. We still keep in touch after all these years, and I told her she was going in the book because I wanted people to know the help she gave me. And yes, Judy is still sober, loving life, and thanking God for the precious gift he gave her.

People assume alcoholics live under bridges and drink from brown paper bags. I have met people from all walks of life, including millionaires, doctors, lawyers, and business people and what mankind calls the common people. I knew a woman who was worth tens of millions of dollars and could not stay sober for any length of time. The last time I saw her she was sitting in the corner of a meeting room crying her eyes out, asking why she drank the way she did. The simplest answer I could give her was that is what alcoholics do.

The one thing alcoholics have in common is that we suffer from the bondage of self. Just getting sober does not change your character. If you were a horse thief before, you are still a horse thief when you sober up unless your character changes. The type of change needed is not an easy thing to do alone if it can even be done alone.

There will be religious people who say you need only to pray, for the Bible says you are a new creation in God when you ask him to forgive you (2 Cor. 5:17 NKJV). I think those people have never been addicted to anything more than having two bowls of ice cream. Yes God spiritually changes you when you pray, asking for help and forgiveness. But there is still the body we live in, and that is what gives us trouble and must be brought under control. I have seen some where this happened immediately, but for the most part it is a process that continues up to the day we die.

The rooms we met in back then were smoke filled. Once in a while the door would be open to the outside, and all you would see would be a smoke cloud escaping from within. I would not have gone back if I had been told I couldn't smoke at the first meeting I went to. I was a chain smoker, smoking around five packs of cigarettes a day. I didn't like anyone telling me what to do, and I believe that would have been the straw that broke the camel's back.

A man I went to for advice often was Chuck Peterson. He came from the same walk of life as I did in that he worked in construction, was divorced, and was a combat veteran. Having been in both the Korean War and the

Vietnam War, we talked the same language. He never cut me slack, always telling me what he thought was the truth and what he would do in a situation, but he never told me what I should do. He was trustworthy, and I valued his friendship very much. He died awhile back from lung cancer and pneumonia.

Whenever I am in McFarland, Michigan, I stop in and see Chuck at the cemetery. I took my thirty-year-old daughter over to his grave when we had a funeral for a member of Deb's family. I told her how this man had helped me stay sober and the respect I had for him.

Chuck had a buddy in the air force, and when they were discharged, they both stayed in Marquette because Chuck was originally from the area. Chuck's buddy also had a drinking problem, and after getting sober, he became an alcohol counselor at the treatment center. He always laughed at people who went back to drinking and then returned after a few days because they ran out of money. He said he would do it differently, and he did. The day he decided he wanted to drink more than he wanted to stay sober, he went to the bank, taking out one thousand dollars, and after that he walked across the street to a bar. I don't remember if he ever made it back. That was too bad because he helped a lot of people get sober.

Chapter 22

I walked into the meeting place one night when I heard all this laughter coming from the kitchen. As I rounded the corner, looking down this long hallway into the kitchen, I saw a young woman sitting on the heat radiator. She glanced my way but didn't seem too impressed with what she saw. I didn't want to take my eyes off her and kept glancing at her as everyone talked. I thought she was the prettiest woman in the room. She said she was coming for another type of meeting that met there because she thought her boyfriend had a drinking problem. We talked for a little bit, and then the meetings started.

Other than her looks, the thing I remember most was her smile and huge Afro. She said it was a permanent, but if it looks like an Afro, it's an Afro. Her name was Debby. She was nineteen years old and was living with Gail, the ex-wife of a friend who got sober and then was killed in a traffic accident in Florida. Gail and I went out for a while, and when I went to visit, Deb was always there. The relationship with Gail broke off, but Deb and I continued to see one another.

Deb would occasionally come over or I would stop by her place, and we'd talk about what was happening in our lives. She had this innocence about her and was intriguing and fun to be with. The image of her sitting on that radiator is still with me thirty-seven years later. She grew up with Chuck's niece Judy, spending the summers with them. Deb would go down to Wind Lake, Wisconsin, once in a while because that was where her folks lived. Her grandparents, Jorma and Elsie Syrjanen, started the Trenary Bakery, which became well known for its Trenary toast. Her Grandmother Celia Englund owned the bar at McFarland, Michigan, and she had relatives in Rock and Skandia, Michigan. I thought about her a lot more than she knew and always looked forward to seeing her.

In November of 1976, I traveled to Midland, Michigan, for Thanksgiving. I was like the prodigal son coming home, only this time I was sober. While there I went to Saginaw to see Mom. They were living in a very rough section of town now, with lots of shootings and stabbings. Duane answered the door, leading me into the living room. It was a dark apartment, which didn't surprise me. Mom was sitting in a big recliner with a sixteen ounce bottle of beer between her legs. She looked rough and was really bloated from her drinking.

We sat in the living room making small talk for a while, and then I started to tell her what had happened in my life since March 21. She listened to what I said, drinking from the bottle every now and then. She was glad that my life had turned around, but she had tried living sober and wanted nothing more to do with it. There was not anything further to say so I left, knowing she was not in a good place. She knew it was going to get worse, and so did I.

I spent a couple of days around Midland and then headed for Marquette. It is a four-and-half-hour-trip, and

I thought about what had happened at Mom's and what the outcome would be. But sad to say, there was nothing I could do just as no one could do anything when I was there. Life was what life was, and I had to accept it. As soon as I got to Marquette, I called some people, and we met at a meeting that night. It felt good to be around folks who were going in the same direction I was.

Just before Christmas, Carol called and said Mom was in the hospital. Her liver was giving her problems, and it looked like she wasn't going to live through it. I called the hospital, talking to Mom for a few moments, and at the end of the conversation, I told her I loved her and she said the same to me. Then she said she was tired and had to go. That would be the last time we talked.

When I hung up the phone I called Butch, telling him what was going on. He had not had any contact with Mom for quite some time because he didn't want his family to be around the drinking. Butch had quit drinking years before after suffering anxiety attacks. Sue and Butch were deeply involved in the church, and that involvement kept him sober. He stated later he was glad I called because he and Mom had a good talk and were able to put things behind them.

A few days later I got a call from my ex-wife, asking if I could come into town because she wanted to talk. It was snowing out, but I figured what the heck and headed to Marquette. Ten minutes after I got there, the phone rang, and Butch told me Mom had passed away. I knew it was coming, but it was still a shock. They wanted me around someone before they told me for fear of I would go back to the bottle. Peg said she wanted to ride down so I told her to plan on leaving the next day.

When I got home, I called some people from the meetings, telling them what was happening. Don told me to take it easy and when I walked up to the casket to remember but for God's grace that could be me lying there. I don't remember much about what happened during the wake, but I remember walking into Taylor's Funeral Home and looking at Mom in the casket. I knew if I ever went back to the bottle that would be me lying there. Mom didn't look good because of the bloat, and there was no doubt she had lived a hard life and it finally caught up to her.

Duane spent a lot of money on the funeral, or so his mother said, and she was not happy about it. I remember her telling Butch, Carol, and I that it was a sin to spend the amount of money Duane spent. This was the same woman who called up Grandma Spencer before she died and the two of them would stick their two cents into everyone's business. I told her that the sin in God's sight would be to forget the love they had for each other and the money meant nothing. She apparently didn't like that because she stayed away from me the rest of the funeral. I was a pallbearer at Mom's funeral, and she was placed in the ground on December 24, 1976, being buried next to her parents, sister, and one brother. Grandma and Grandpa Spencer and their son Leon are buried across the walkway. I spent Christmas day with family and then went back to Marquette a few days later.

Once again I got back into my routine of work, meetings, and hanging out with people from the meetings. I heard that Deb and Gail were having a New Year's Eve party at their place. I talked to Dave, a buddy of mine, and we decided to go to it. This was a very small house, and by the time we got there, the place was packed. I found Deb, and she was upset because she had no idea who most of the people there were. She also was worried about some money she had stashed in her bedroom because there were people everywhere.

We went to her bedroom, where she hid the money in a safer place, and then we went for a walk. She was really upset about all the people so I told her if it would help, I would spend the night. She said it would. We woke up the next morning and saw people sprawled everywhere. It didn't look as if anyone had gone home, just staying where they dropped.

Something happened between us that night because we saw each other almost daily after that. She likes to tell people that I drove by her house very slow on the way home from work, and within fifteen minutes, she would receive a phone call from me. I don't remember it that way, but as usual with everything else, she is probably right. I do remember that she came over on a regular basis for home-cooked meals. She was fun to be with and had such an energy for life it amazed me. I would stare at her when she wasn't looking for I always thought she was the prettiest woman in the room, always wondering why she was with someone like me.

February 1, 1977

To have compassion for someone who has wronged you and to pray for that person is commendable. But to feel it with all your heart and very being is an act of God. I believe it is his way of telling you that things are okay and for us to get busy with our own lives and to turn our problems over to him. He is the only one who is truly capable of understanding them, and in turn, he is the only one who can do anything about them. It is not for me to try to understand why or how things happened. It is only for me to try to grow into what God wants me to be. And the only way I can do this is by saying, "Here, God, I can't deal with this so would you take it and do with it what you will?" It is my choice on what I want to become or do in this life. God has given me the choice. But if I remember where it was exactly I came from then it really isn't a choice at all because I know for certain I don't want to go back to that life I left eleven months ago. With all of its hate, fears, and loneliness, it was a very sad world.

In May of 1977, Deb called to say she was coming over. When she got there, I could see she was troubled by something. I was sitting in a green chair by the window, and she was sitting on the floor next to me. That is when the world as I knew it changed forever.

She told me she was pregnant, and after talking about it for a while, like a complete idiot, I asked her if she was certain the baby was mine. Typical male remark! I knew the answer because we never left one another's sight. It was like I slapped her when I said that, and I can still see the hurt and confused look on her face. I told her I didn't want to get married but would help in any way I could. It is hard for me to write this because I realize how hurt she must have felt and how abandoned.

She left to go back to her place, and my mind was racing a mile a minute. Looking back it had nothing to do with Deb or the baby, but the fact was I didn't know if I was grown up enough to take on the responsibility. I talked to her I believe the next day, and she said she was moving back to Wind Lake. We talked a few more times, and then she was gone.

I went over to Chuck Peterson's a few days later, telling him what had happened. He was sitting at his kitchen table drinking coffee as I sat down across from him. After getting it all out, I looked to him for some sort of advice, but all he did was put a big smile on his face while reaching across the table to shake my hand, telling me congratulations.

You could have knocked me over with a feather when he did that. I wanted to scream, "Can't you see how serious this is!" In his wisdom, he knew exactly how serious it was but also knew it wasn't worth getting drunk over and that it would work out. Chuck cared as much if not more for Deb as he did for me, but not once did he tell me what I should do. He knew I had to come to it by myself with God's help and that would take time.

I went to even more meetings and talked to everyone who would listen. I was going to be a father but didn't know if I could take care of myself, let alone a wife and baby. I started to work a lot of hours to take my mind off it, sometimes getting to meetings after they started. There were times when I fell asleep at the meeting I was so tired, but I knew I was safe there from taking a drink. Deb and the baby were on my mind constantly for the next eleven months.

I wrote this on September 4, 1977:

A light of love and peace came to me. With understanding and compassion, it spoke to me in a way of knowing. It was not really a voice but a thought. Before my question was even formed, I had the answer. It said, "I am the God of your fathers. I am the one you seek. Lift up your heart, for I am with you. My strength and love flow into you, and we are as one. Rejoice in your sorrow, for I am the resurrection. Yea though you walk through the valley, I am with you." Then the voice left but is still with me. It's that voice of all knowing and all caring. My hand trembles as I write this, but it is of expectation and not of fear.

I had no contact with Deb until late March, when I received a subpoena from the Racine County District Attorney in Wisconsin telling me to report there on a certain date. I called information for Racine, getting the number of an attorney, and set up a time to meet him. I went down the day before and met with the people they told me to meet. Unknown to me there was also a warrant out for my arrest that went along with the subpoena; so I was arrested and handcuffed, which surprised the heck out of me because there were so many other things I should have been arrested for. Then they took me to another room, took off the cuffs, and told me to report to another office the next day.

I was at a meeting that night, and first thing the next morning I went and saw the lawyer. We met in a local bar because he was between cases. After I told him what was happening, he said he would be at the meeting in the afternoon. The lawyer and I met at one o'clock and went to the meeting.

When we were led into the room, Deb was sitting with a caseworker and assistant district attorney. We looked at each other, and there was still that magic I felt when I looked at her. I sat down across from her, and could hardly keep my eyes off her. Afterward we went to a restaurant for lunch and she slid a picture of my son across to me. He was adorable! I realized he was part of me and this beautiful women sitting across from me, making him really special.

Deb said she had named him Josh, which was what I always wanted my son to be named. The assistant district attorney and caseworker began to ask questions of Deb, with her relating her side of it, and then we broke for recess. My lawyer told me that there was no way anyone was going to side with me. If he had to vote for Deb or me he would vote for Deb. I don't think he fully understood because I never wanted to get out of anything, just to have it done properly.

We went back to the meeting and were told they would get in touch with us once a court date was set. We left, heading for the parking lot together and going to my car to talk. Then one thing led to another, and we were soon making out in broad daylight in the parking lot of the Racine County Courthouse. She likes to say I started it, but it was her, for she never could keep her hands off me. I said I would call her as soon as I got home.

We talked every day, and she told me she would be coming up to Skandia within a week and her cousin Jeff would bring her and Josh over, but I would have to take them back to her aunt's house. She called a couple days later, saying they were at Skandia and would be over in a little while.

I heard the car come into the driveway, hurrying to the door to meet them. It was snowing a little, and she had the baby bundled up tight. The first thing she did was put him into my arms! After she took her coat off, she started to take him out of his blankets and snow suit. When his face came into view, my heart broke into a thousand pieces. I could not believe something so precious had come from me.

We sat and talked for a couple of hours while I held Josh most of the time. The whole time they were there felt right, like that was the way it was supposed to be. It was getting late, and she needed to get back to her aunt's, so off we went into the night.

I remember walking into her aunt's house and this blond woman came rushing up and taking Josh out of my arms. It seemed to me that she was checking Josh over, making sure I had not done anything to him. I felt like telling her to kiss off but kept my mouth shut. Deb introduced me to her mother (the blond women), Aunt Louise, and Uncle Tom.

We went outside and talked for a while, hugging each other good-bye. I told Deb I would be calling her within a day or two and to start packing for the move to Marquette. I didn't tell her, but the week before I was going down the road talking with God about what to do, and he said three words: "Marry the woman." There was a sudden and complete peace that came over me as God spoke this to me, so I knew before Deb came up that would be the way it was to be. I have never regretted marrying her and would do it all over again, only this time it would be before she got pregnant.

Chapter 23

I called Chuck, telling him what was happening and what we were going to do. He said it was a good choice and that if I needed any help to let him know. I called Deb, and we talked about when would be a good time to come and get her and Josh. We had a court meeting in a week, so we decided we would do it then. During that week I tried getting used to other people living with me by leaving stuff laying around the house and not keeping it as clean as I was used to. I had become a clean freak after I sobered up and knew it wouldn't be that way with another person and a baby living there. Apparently I did not acclimate myself very well because I would make Deb mad when I came home from work as I was always picking up little things. She told me later one day she scrubbed the house from top to bottom, and when I walked in the door that night, instead of a compliment for what she had done, I leaned over and picked a piece of dog hair off the rug. She should have smacked me with a skillet upside of the head.

I was looking over my writings, and I found one I wrote in March of 1978. It made sense for where I was and what was going on in my life. I wrote this on March 1, 1978:

With acceptance comes the serenity to move forward. The war within is at peace, and you are as one with the universe. The ever-conflicting fears, anger, and doubt are no more. Your spirit flies on the wind and laughs with the happiness of a child . . . It is being born again, with total trust toward that which is all love and ever giving. The joy of this is given unto all but lived by only a few. To receive such a beautiful gift is done by nothing more than a willingness to open the heart. As each new day breaks forth, may I seek the willingness to accept the gift.

The following week I headed for Wind Lake, Wisconsin, to pick up Deb and Josh. Once I got there, it took several phone calls to find her folks' store because I was on one end of this road and they lived on the other. When I got close, I could see Deb on the patio above the store. She waved as I pulled into the parking lot and was coming through the back door as I walked up to it. We hugged and kissed for a minute when she said the words I didn't want to hear: "Come in and I will introduce you to my family." I met her mother once more and her dad as I walked in the back door since they were working that day. We went upstairs where they lived and talked for a while, and then the two of them went back to work. Her older brother, Doug, with his wife, Cindy, stopped by later. We checked the phone book for trailer rentals and ended up renting a U-Haul.

The following day we went to Racine and talked with the caseworker and assistant district attorney involved in the case. We explained to them Deb would be moving to

Michigan and that we were getting married. They said that was fine with them, but they told me they had better not see any litigation with my name on it again concerning this case. Everyone wants the last word. Years later I put high-speed data lines into this same courthouse and knew the county executive personally. We spent the rest of the day packing and were planning to leave first thing in the morning. Later that night her dad told me that he didn't like me much when all of this first started. I told him that was understandable but I hoped we could get along in the future, but that would end up being elusive.

We left the next morning, arriving back in Harvey, Michigan, by late afternoon. Harvey is approximately four miles south of Marquette on M-28. As soon as we were unpacked, June 3 was chosen for the wedding date. I had a friend who was managing a jewelry store, and he said to come in to look at what he had to offer. When we arrived, he had already laid out some rings for Deb to look at. Deb liked one in particular so that was the one we purchased.

There was a small church on M-28 just down from our house so we called the pastor to make an appointment to talk with him. He was a young guy in his mid-thirties and seemed like he knew what he was talking about in the beginning. The more we talked, though, the more of what he said didn't make sense. He thought it would be better if we lived together for a year before getting married to see if we were compatible.

We looked at one another, not believing what this so-called man of God was telling us. We both knew what he was saying was wrong, and we told him in no uncertain terms that was not going to happen and if he didn't want to perform the wedding we would go somewhere else.

After more discussion, he stated that he would perform the ceremony. There were no marriage classes back then like there are now so all we had was the rehearsal and then the wedding itself.

Dave, the guy I went to Deb's New Year's Eve party with, was my best man, and Carol, a friend of Deb's from Wisconsin, was her bridesmaid. Her Aunt Louise and Uncle Tom said they would have a reception at their house the afternoon of the wedding. The day of the wedding was a warm, sunny day. Sometime during the wedding Josh, who was being held by Louis, threw up, spraying the woman who was sitting directly behind them. For some reason Louise thought that was cute and laughed about it whenever it was brought up. Strange woman!

Deb's grandmother Elsie had a good friend who was a member of the church and was not happy when she found out what the pastor told us about living together for a year. I would not have wanted to be in his shoes when that sweet old lady got a hold of him. Butch and Sue with their two children came up for the wedding. I had not seen them for some time, and it was good to talk with them. I told them we would be coming to Midland in a few weeks so Deb could meet the rest of the family. It was a nice reception and also the first time I ever tasted brats. They were made by Deb's dad, who was a meat cutter by trade and really knew how to work a piece of meat. I thought they would have been good with a beer, but that was out of the question. I found it amazing that I went through this whole episode without taking or thinking about a drink. The old Phil would have been drunk from day one.

We went home that night as a married couple with a small baby starting our lives together. It wasn't long before I started to act like an idiot. Most of the despicable things in my character started to come to the surface, and Deb said later that she often wondered what she had gotten herself and Josh into. I went back to working a lot of overtime, which was good for me because it kept my mind occupied, but it never occurred to me how much I was leaving Deb home alone. My mind was telling me that I was supplying my family with the things they needed to live on when in reality I was stealing from them the time I should have been spending with them.

One day I was putting wood shakes around the front door when the ladder didn't do what I wanted it to. I went nuts, throwing the ladder out into the middle of the front yard along with a few good cuss words following it. I looked at Deb, who was standing there holding Josh and watching me with a shocked look on her face. She told me years later that at that moment, she thought she had married a crazy man.

We visited not only her aunts and uncles often but also her grandparents. They were and are good people, accepting me into the family with open arms, all except her Aunt Louise. There was nothing I could do to please that woman, and she told me if I didn't take care of Deb appropriately, she would bury me somewhere deep in the woods. It got to be a joke between us, but I knew she was serious about that walk in the woods.

When our daughter, Sarah, was in college, she asked Louise why she didn't like me. Louise told Sarah that was the way it was and she needed to accept it and move on. Louise told me later she didn't know what to say because the question shocked her so much. Louise died from cancer on June 17, 2013. She scared a lot of people during her life, but there was a softness and love for her family and friends that will be forever missed.

Deb and I agreed that our marriage and family would be built upon the rock of Jesus and that the children would grow up with him spiritually, not religiously. There have been a lot of storms that have come against it over the years, but it still stands. I will say that 99.9 percent of those storms have come from my actions. For about three months we attended a small church that was meeting on the campus of Northern Michigan University. We also attended a Bible study taught by Vaughn and Terri at their home. Vaughn was the first man who ever asked me what my relationship with Jesus was. I asked Vaughn what I had to give up in my life to follow Christ, and he said nothing. The closer I got to Jesus, the more I would let go of the things I thought of as important now.

Vaughn was very concerned with where people were going to spend eternity. It was brought up in the Bible study that anyone who wished to be baptized by immersion should have it done. Vaughn contacted the Church of Christ in Gwinn, and they set up a Sunday where Vaughn would baptize us. I had been sprinkled as a baby at the Methodist Church in Freeland, Michigan, but this would be complete immersion and meant more to me because it was my outward confession of accepting Christ as my Savior. Deb and I did this together, and I can still see her face as she came out of the water.

As the Bible study grew in number, it was decided as a group that we should look at affiliating with a denominational church. Vaughn sent letters to some denominational churches, and the letters they sent back were the things we would have to do to meet their requirements. Very little of it had to do with the Bible but were rules and regulations in their denomination. We thought better of it and decided to have church at Vaughn and Terri's house every Sunday. We set up a couple of baby cribs, thoroughly enjoying God's Word on a very simple level. Later in life Vaughn wrote a book about alcoholism entitled *From Addiction to Serenity* by Vaughn W. For anyone who wants to understand the twelve-step program that Vaughn wrote about, this would be an excellent book to get. He discusses each step in a very simplistic way.

We made the trip to Midland so Deb could meet the other half of what she had married into. We were at Dad and Barb's for dinner when Joe, my half-brother, screwed up calling Deb by my first wife's name. Deb handled it better than I did. I told Joe afterward I didn't appreciate it and never to let it happen again. This was the first time Deb met Carol and her family. Deb got along well with everyone, but as we stayed at Butch's, I think she got closer to Sue on this visit.

I believe it was the first or second time we went to Midland, and on the way back, my insanity flared up again. Josh had been crying for about twenty miles and my nerves were shot when I started ranting and raving at Deb to make him shut up. It was another one of my memorable moments. I would have more than my share of them over the next sixteen years. Why Deb stayed with me is an act of God because she probably would have been happier if she had pulled the plug and found someone else.

I was not a happy camper for a very long time. It had nothing to do with being married because I liked and wanted to be married. It had to do with my inability to be at peace with myself or the world around me. It is amazing how you see something one way and someone else sees it differently. For me I had the funnel turned, looking at life through the big end into the small and not the small into the big. There is no way you can get the right perspective on life if you don't see the big picture, and I didn't even know there was a picture. I was going to meetings but still was a mess when it came to my thinking. For some reason when everything is going good in alcoholics' lives, we like to throw a wrench in it just to screw it up. We say we don't but we love chaos and will do whatever it takes to get it going.

One winter's night we were on our way to Grandpa John and Grandma Elsie's, and they were talking about Elvis Presley dying on the radio. I mentioned to Deb that it would be nice if the Lord came right then and we could go home to heaven. There were big snowflakes falling, and I remember Deb saying she didn't want to leave because she wanted to raise Josh and enjoy her life as a mother. She wasn't saying no to Jesus but was saying yes to motherhood. It gave me pause for thought, but it was years later before I fully understood what she meant. Like I have been told, I am not the sharpest stick in the wood pile.

We spent a great deal of time at her aunts', uncles', and grandparents' houses. Her uncle Ronnie had a camp over by Gwinn, and we would spend the days out there. Deb always wanted to stay the night, but I wanted nothing to do with camping in any form. There was an outhouse, a hand pump for water, and no electricity, and to me that's camping. I promised myself when I got out of the military that my days of living that way were over. Deb at times would stay all night with Josh and her relatives.

There was the traditional July 4 celebration where everyone went out to Ronnie's camp to pitch horseshoes, eat, and drink some beers. Being around the drinking never bothered me out there. They were good times, and they continue to this day. Even after we moved Deb and the kids would go back for it almost every year. We had been hoping for another baby, so when we found out Deb was pregnant, we were elated. I wanted to have three children, but Deb wanted two. Years later when both kids were grown and out of the house, she said she wished we had had another. I wrote the following over the next few months:

September 3, 1978

As the sea gently rolls its waves onto the sands of time, may your life be brought to new horizons; with the strength and love of our Lord flowing from you to all that passes your way! May those who receive also in his name give, for it is in this life that we prepare ourselves for that which was, is, and shall be throughout eternity.

September 2, 1978

In the solitude of prayer lies the answer to life, but the answer may not be thy will but that of the giver. What a revelation in the moment of oneness.

September 2, 1978

The heart that cries with mankind is a heart warmed by God's love!

I continued to go to meetings and thought I was getting better in both my actions and thinking. I was to some extent, but I also had not let go of most of my past, and some things I wouldn't know were there until much later in life. It was a time of personal growth but also a time of false pride and denial of my emotional and spiritual stability. I thought I had arrived, but unknown to me, I was supposed to have taken a boat but found myself on a train. I was starting to think I had a few answers at the meetings I went to, and that went right to my head. The one thing I knew beyond anything was that I loved the wife God had given me, the child we had, and the one on the way. I was terrible at showing and expressing that love, and that would be something I would struggle with the rest of my life.

I was elected president of the local Communications Workers of America union in Marquette, so I had a direct line to the assistant vice president of Michigan Bell. For some reason I hit it off with him and my division manager, who was a Christian. Being president of the local gave me access to a lot of people I would normally not have come in contact with. That again would become a pride issue that I would not become aware of until later in life.

One of the people I dealt with directly was the state director of the CWA International. His name was Dan Carr, and he was an honorable and decent man. He knew a lot about people having problems with alcohol and would always ask how it was going. We had a district meeting in Cleveland, Ohio, one time, and Dan told me he had a job for me when I got there. It turned out the job was to be the bartender in the hospitality room. I ask him if he had gone nuts, but he said I needed to get used to being around it and there was no better time than now. It proved to be a very good lesson for me, and I would use that experience in the future. That doesn't mean I started hanging out in the bars, but it did give me the ability to go into one if I had to.

Dan and his wife came up to Marquette to visit, and Deb and I met them for dinner. His wife chewed on us when we got there because we came on my motorcycle. She asked one question and that was what would happen to Josh if we were killed on the bike? We had no answer for that so had to make arrangements to ensure Josh was taken care of.

Later I called Connie, president of the Saginaw local, asking if she could get the bigger local's downstate to meet at Mackinaw City without the international being present. She was able to do so, and we all met there to discuss issues we were having with both the company and the international. A few of the international representatives tried to come to the meeting and were told in no uncertain terms that it would be healthier for them if they didn't. We left that meeting with an understanding that if you messed with one local, you messed with them all. If I had a problem in Marquette, the word went out and every local got involved at their locations.

I remember one time we were at a state meeting when there were some problems with the operators in Grand Rapids, and they walked off the job. The company fixed it by by-passing Grand Rapids and sending everything to Lansing. Lansing walked also, and the international came to the meeting and told the local presidents to put everyone back to work. We told them to kiss off and that if the company and international didn't fix the problem we would put the whole state out on the street. It took them about half an hour to fix the problem.

That was one thing that came out of the meeting in Mackinaw City, and I found out later that because of the close work between the locals, the state went to a one-tier pay scale. It is amazing what can happen when a strong union stands its ground for the right issues. Sad to say, by the time I retired it was not that way. I did a lot of traveling for the local, and it was a fun time to be involved. I tried to get involved with the union in Wisconsin, but they were not of the same caliber as Michigan.

Deb was depressed from the moment she moved back to the Upper Peninsula. Even though her aunts and uncles lived close by, she felt alone. There was no one her age to talk to or do things with. Since we only had one car for a while, the feeling of isolation overwhelmed her. We later got a pickup truck so that made it a little better, but she still was lonely. She lost some of that as we got involved with the Bible studies and church, but it never fully left.

Then there was the thing of living in a house your husband had built with his former wife. I was brain dead when it came to these things and never gave it a thought because I was busy earning a living while going to meetings four times a week. I was doing the things I thought a proper husband and father should do for his family. What an idiot! The most important thing I should have been doing was to make sure my wife's emotional wellbeing was cared for.

Deb began to talk about moving so naturally I thought she meant to Wisconsin, but I found out twenty-five years later that she just wanted to move from the house we were living in. Talk about a lack of communication. So without really knowing what the wife wanted I put in a transfer. After one year the transfer was automatically pulled, and sure enough, on the last day I received a call from the transfer bureau. They had an opening in Madison, Wisconsin, and wanted to know if I would take it. I talked with Deb that night and she said to take the job.

In 1980, with Deb eight months pregnant, we put the house up for sale and headed to Wisconsin. Her folks said we could live with them until we found a place to buy, but we did not know they also had her other brother and his wife living there. Her brother Doug had a friend who worked for a moving company, and they picked up our stuff, storing it at their warehouse. It was decided I would use her parents' camper to live in during the week but that didn't work out because there were no camp sites close, so I drove three hours a day from Wind Lake to Madison.

With the driving, three families living in the same house, and me not going to meetings, I was emotionally and spiritually bankrupt. Her folks lived above the grocery store they owned so there was always chaos. The one thing that set me off more than anything else was everyone had a habit of leaving meat-cutting knives lying around. Josh was old enough by now to be getting into everything and I didn't want those knifes lying out. I had more than one argument with them on this point.

I learned from this living arrangement that you do not put a recovering alcoholic under the same roof with two other families, especially when some of them drink. I wouldn't say all the chaos was my fault but enough of it was. One day Deb and I got in a bad argument, and I told her I was leaving. Well about three miles down the road it dawned on me that I had no place to go and didn't know anyone in the area, so with my head down, I went back and made amends to Deb. I never was known for my brain working before my mouth.

I want to say that it was more than a lot of parents would have done for their daughter, letting us live there for the year we did, and I want to thank them for that. I believe it was during this time frame that Deb's parents began to dislike me, and it has been that way for more than thirty-five years. We have different values, and those values don't go together. It is like oil and water; they just don't mix. Deb and I have always believed that God comes before anything else where they wanted no part of God. Deb's dad thinks God does not exist. I would like to say that I was a good example of what Christ wants us to be, but just the opposite was true. I was in the middle of a dry drunk that made life unbearable for my wife, son, and soon-to-be daughter and everyone else I came in contact with. The only thing that was missing was the alcohol.

L-R Phil—Butch & Carol Spencer
Date unknown

Front Row L-R Butch—Carol & Phil
Back Row L-R Dad & Mom
1956

Front Row L—R Mom & Marion Brewster
Back Row L—R Grandpa Brewster & Grandma Brewster
1940

Grandma & Grandpa Spencer with Rex
1964

Duane & Mom—1969

Phil in Vietnam 1968

Phil in 1972

**Deb & Phil's Wedding
1978**

Phil climbing a pole—57 years old 2004

Stewie on the stairs—2008

I wrote this on January 24, 1980:

Into the nail-scarred hands of Jesus I place my soul. Into the strong, weathered hands of the true Healer who molded wood as a young man and healed the infirmities of mankind during his ministry. The hands that supported our cross as he walked his last walk on earth. Into these same hands that tenderly held a child, I place my soul. With a tear of happiness, I pray for him to mold me into what he would have me be. I pray he would lift me unto the mountaintops and plunge me into the cleansing of his grace. Oh to walk by him and to hold those hands. To have him brush away the tears of this world while taking my hand in prayer and praise unto the Father. Unto you, Jesus, the living Son of the living Father, the beginning and end, I commend my soul.

Amen.

Shortly after we moved to Wisconsin, Deb went into labor, and we headed to the Menomonee Falls Hospital. It was an hour trip to the hospital from Wind Lake, and we left at about 11:30 at night. I don't remember the labor being that long, but Deb might have a different opinion. It was there that our daughter Sarah came into this world. She had the biggest blue eyes I had ever seen and was as cute as a button. Our little family was now complete. I remember walking out of the elevator as we took her home a couple of days later, and this older couple could not get over how blue her eyes were.

Right then and there I should have made arrangements to move the family to another house where we would have been by ourselves, but I didn't and would later regret it. Now there were four people living in this ten-by-ten-foot room with two dogs. Shortly after we took her home from the hospital, she threw up, getting some vomit down her windpipe. It was back to the hospital only this time at Burlington with Deb staying at Sarah's side until she was discharged. It was heartbreaking to see her tiny body lying in the hospital bed knowing there is nothing you can do. I experienced this with both kids while they were growing up. It is a horrifying feeling to be totally helpless when it comes to one of your children. It was a good day when she came out of there.

I drove back and forth to Madison for a couple of months, and then Wisconsin Bell moved me closer to where Deb and the kids were. It was only temporary duty, but at least I was getting closer. Finally I was transferred to Lake Geneva, which is about twenty miles southwest of Wind Lake. Deb started to look for a place to buy before I went nuts, finding a nice piece of property in rural Burlington. We hired a contractor to rough in the house, finishing the rest of the house ourselves. Deb's dad did all the wiring, saving us a bunch of money, and Deb and I pretty much did the rest.

Deb and I were at the house working one day when I heard Josh yelling for help. We found him with half of his body sticking out of the driveway culvert. It's a good thing his clothes got caught because I don't know how we would have gotten him out if he had made it all the way in. I drove a steel post at both ends so he wasn't able to repeat that.

Deb would have really been upset if she had known what was going through my mind regarding a guy at work. He thought he was the center of the universe and was one of the most obnoxious, self-centered, arrogant individuals I had ever been around. He went behind people's backs, talking to management about them, trying to make himself look better at the expense of others. He could not have cared less about how much trouble he caused in people's lives.

I finally had it one day when he got me in trouble with the foreman. The guy needed to be eliminated, and I knew just how to do it. The very day I was going to take him out he didn't show up because he got promoted to management, which removed him from the crew. That is the only thing that saved that man from being removed from this world. You can screw with alcoholic for just so long, and then they will find a solution to the problem. It might not be the correct one, but it will be a solution. Looking back I believe that God had everything to do with me not eliminating the guy. He will never know how close he came. This would have been in the middle of 1980. I had not dealt with my rage yet, and it showed.

Chapter 24

During this time, I was not going to meetings, and my thinking and actions got worse by the day. Deb remembers a time when we were coming back from working on the house, and she said how pretty the clouds were that evening. I told her the clouds sucked and why was she looking at the clouds anyway. Yeah, I was a real swell guy, and if you didn't believe me, just ask. Whatever anyone would do, I had an opinion about it. It made no difference if I even knew them. I always tried to raise myself up by putting other people down. I heard of a meeting starting at the Wind Lake Lutheran Church, and I began to go there whenever they met, which was once a week. It was like a breath of fresh air back in my lungs after a long absence. I am not going to say I got sane, but I do think my attitude got just a little better.

This is where I met the first of many people with AIDS. You didn't hear about it back then like you do now. The woman said she had come back to the area of her birth to die. She was extremely attractive at about twenty-five years old but died a horrible death a number of years later in a county home. She had left the area, going out east *to* start her life's journey, but it was not to be. She never told us how she contacted the blood disease, as she referred to it, but she did not look like drug users do when they come in from the street. She was not the last one I would see die of AIDS as more and more people started to come to the meetings with dual addictions.

After we moved to Burlington, I met a man who became a good friend. His name was Vinnie, and he was from New York City, where he became infected with AIDS by using someone else's needle. He came to Burlington to live with his sister until he got his life back together. He remained sober and clean while in Burlington and a few years later went back to New York. With what time he had remaining, he went back to the streets, helping addicts and drunks out of the lifestyle that was killing them. While he was caring for the lost and hopeless, he fell in love with a woman and got married.

Vinnie stayed on the streets helping until he was no longer able to as AIDS took its final toll on his body. His sister told me there were a large number of people who got sober and clean and came to know Jesus through Vinnie's work on the streets of New York City. What a testimony of one man's love for his fellow human beings. There are a lot of religious people who could learn the meaning of love and giving of oneself from him. Sad to say, most of them think they are the only ones that have the right to carry the message of God's grace.

I remember going to the Burlington Hospital to visit a man I did not know but who wanted to talk to someone about his addiction. Another man and I went to see him, and the guy was not in good shape. God spoke to me, telling me to touch the man while I was talking to him. After talking to him, we said a prayer and left. I got a call the next morning saying the man had died during the night of complications from AIDS. I believe Jesus will use whoever to reach people, and a lot of times he uses the very people society has rejected. Praise to God!

The house was finally finished, and we moved in toward the end of 1981. I was not fit to live with by then as my attitude just sucked. The booze wasn't there but everything else was as far as my thoughts and actions. I was a loaded cannon waiting to go off on anyone I came in contact with. I started going to meetings in Burlington shortly after we moved to the house. There were a couple of older guys named Pappy and Dick sitting there as I walked through the door the first time, and when they saw me, they chuckled in that knowing way. It took about six months of going to meetings before I started to think somewhat normally, only to find out twelve years later that I was wrong about that also. It's hard to grow up when you are in an adult body but your mind and emotions are still at the childhood level. I believe when I started to drink I stopped maturing and didn't start again until I quit drinking. That might not make sense to some, but for those who have been there, they know what I mean.

About a year after I got back to meetings I met a guy named Paul, and our backgrounds were almost identical. He worked for the power company, was divorced, spent time in Korea and Vietnam, and would find out later he had PTSD. We both got busted from sergeant E-5. Over the years we have never cut each other slack when it came to honesty about staying sober. I remember one time I called him whining about something, and I sure didn't like what he told me. But after I thought about it for a time, he was right and cared enough about me to let me know.

He lives in Missouri now, but we still maintain contact, stopping in to see each other every now and then.

We received word that Butch's wife, Sue, had cancer. She went in to have a breast removed, and the results looked good for a while. About four years later, the cancer came back with a vengeance. It spread through her body like wildfire, and there was nothing the doctors seemed able to do about it. We went there as often as we could. I remember one time we were there and Sue was feeling better and able to get around somewhat. Deb, Butch, Sue and I were sitting in their living room discussing religion at a time when Sue knew she was dying of cancer. She looked me in the eye and said, "Phil, I don't want to die," but we both knew she was and I didn't have an answer for her.

She had been anointed with oil and prayed over time and again. She had the faith that God would heal her right up to the end. She was a mother who wanted to see her children grow up, get married, and have children of their own. She wanted to spoil those grandchildren like all grandparents do, and she wanted to grow old with the husband God had given her. But none of this was to be, and at a young age, she had to come to terms with that. I believe Sue was able to, but I don't think Butch ever came to terms with her loss. When she went into the hospital for the last time, I called her every day until Butch picked up the phone one morning saying she was too weak to talk anymore. From then on I called Butch until the day I came home from work and Deb was crying because Sue had passed on that day. I remember Butch standing at Sue's casket, and then he leaned down to kiss her one last time. As he patted her hand, he said, "It's over." I asked him what he meant, and he said the only thing that gave him satisfaction at that moment was the knowledge that the cancer that had taken his beloved wife was also dead. It's all in how you look at it.

Deb and I settled in and started on the road that would take the kids to adulthood. We began to go to a church that met in the basement of the Associated Bank in Burlington. It was a small church, and the people had total love for one another. There was also a Bible study that went from house to house, and everyone enjoyed it. I was on the church board and taught adult Sunday school. In hindsight I find it hard to believe they would have allowed me to sweep the floors, let alone sit on the church board. Everything went well until we decided to put up a building. Then it seemed like personalities took over, and principles were thrown out the window. It became one against another, with pride rearing its ugly head on both sides. We got the building up, but by that time, there were so many hard feelings the animosity could be cut with a knife. The church eventually split, with about half staying and half leaving. We were part of the group that left.

At the same time my friend Bud went to the hospital to have a routine procedure done. They were going to look down his throat to see what this flap of skin was he had hanging there. Bud called me the night before, telling me he didn't have a good feeling about the procedure, but instead of telling him to cancel I told him everything would be okay and not to worry. Bud never came out of the hospital. He died a few days later. Somehow he never received enough oxygen during the procedure, and it fried his brain. Bud was a good husband, father, and friend, and life is just not fair at times. If only I had told him to postpone the procedure. The word *if* is a small word, but it can drive people insane when we try to use it for something that happened in the past, wishing the event would have gone the other way.

There was one night I remember very vividly. We were living in Burlington, and I had just stretched out on the bed to go to sleep. As my head hit the pillow, this sense of peace came over me, with all fear and anxiety leaving my body. I knew beyond a doubt that everything was okay in my little part of the world. I sensed that this was the way life was meant to be, with my final thought being that God loves me. I think of what transpired that night as the sleep of the innocent. It was a remarkable gift that God gave me to enjoy even though I have never had another one. Ever since leaving 'Nam I had never had a normal night's sleep, and I would find out later the PTSD was having its way with me.

The kids grew up doing what all kids do as far as sports, school, and discovering life. The one thing I did even if I could not do anything else was stay involved with them at their sports activities. I coached and umpired Little League and was on the board of the local soccer club, making all their games. Even there my personality, for lack of a better word, would get in the way. I remember one baseball coach from another team telling me to get real, and I told him I would show him what reality was if he wanted. I almost got a red card at a soccer game when some of us parents got into it. Beware of how loudly you yell because your kids can pick out your voice from a thousand. When Sarah was playing soccer, the one thing that kept me level was one of the dads from her team. He was not only a Vietnam veteran but also a detective on the Racine police department and always carried two guns that I knew of. There was no sense in irritating him.

When Josh was in the first grade, we moved him out of the public school system, putting him in St. John's Lutheran School in Burlington until the eighth grade. Sarah would follow two years later. It was a good school and taught the kids a lot of things they would use later in life. They would argue about that and especially one teacher no one seemed to like, including the parents, but I believe this was where they got their studying skills that saw them through the rest of their schooling.

There were a number of things that took place while the kids were growing to adulthood that I wish I could redo. I thought I was this perfect husband and father, but that was not the case. I will say that sometimes you have to be beat down pretty good to look at yourself. Who wants to admit they are a hemorrhoid? There were times when there was not enough Preparation H to stop the swelling of my ego.

The kids would have been about eight and six years old when this happened. We were eating supper when Deb said something, and I opened my mouth, saying if she didn't know what she was talking about she should keep her mouth shut. It was like I slapped her, and out the door she went. I can still see the hurt look on her face and the kids wondering what had just happened. I figured she would walk it off, but an hour later she wasn't back and I was getting worried. I went looking for her but I couldn't find her until after several trips around the neighborhood I finally saw her at a neighbor's house that was being renovated.

I always said things I shouldn't, and I always went straight for the throat. Even though I had stopped drinking years before, I was not a pleasant person to be around. I was mean, opinionated, and combative and always had to be right. If the world would only do what I wanted it to, everything would be okay. Was I this way all the time? Of course not, but I could and would step over that invisible line at a moment's notice.

As I said before, we were involved with a number of churches, helping build one from a vacant lot to a nice building only to see it split later. During this time I began to realize that church people are just as screwed up as drunks and drug addicts, only they call it by other names. I thought I had arrived and was this upstanding member of the community, only to discover I was still a scumbag. I was living in the same body I had when I was out there using and abusing, and it did what it wanted to whenever it wanted to. Pride kills everything you hold dear, and what is so cunning about it is you don't know it has you until it is too late.

I was walking around with my head in the so-called heavenly clouds not understanding that I was one big, open sore to everyone around me. Walk in humility before the Lord God or you will fall in your pride. I know this to be true because I did it over and over in my life. You would have thought somewhere along the road it would have sunk in.

Sarah told her mom she wished I could work all the time, for that would keep me out of the house and I wouldn't cause all the chaos I did. I was sixteen years sober when Deb told me I had a year to clean up my act or I was out of the house. She was tired of my anger and the way I was around her and the kids. I remember sitting in the basement on a couch when Sarah came by and asked me what was wrong, for I looked like I had lost my best friend. I told her I had, forcing back tears.

Remember, all these thought processes came from my alcoholic thinking. Just because you put away the bottle doesn't mean you are cured. It takes the rest of your life to clean out the garbage your mind has stored in it. It took about nine months of one-on-one counseling for me to let go of my rage. That has been years ago, and up to now I have not had a problem with it coming back. I discovered I had life wrapped around me too tightly, and it was strangling me.

I replaced the rage with my own brand of off color humor, and it has worked for me up to this point. I am not talking about vulgar humor but stuff that sometimes just doesn't make any sense no matter how you look at it. Years later I was told I used humor to escape from reality and I should stop doing that. I admit that my humor can be bizarre sometimes as far as being politically incorrect, and most normal people do not understand it. What do they want me to do, go back to allowing the rage to control me? They would not like that person. The people at the meetings and where I volunteer accept me for what and who I am, and that is good enough.

Josh got involved with soccer at St. John's and continued it into high school. He was also part of the Burlington Soccer Club, traveling to other towns to play. He received three varsity letters in high school, and they took first place at sectionals I believe on three different occasions. His club team took first place in their conference and second place at the Badger State Games. He went to the

University of Lacrosse in Lacrosse, Wisconsin, acquiring a BS in biology and a masters in molecular and cellular biology. Then while employed by the Mayo Clinic, in Rochester Minnesota, he received a master's in business administration. He married a girl he met while in college, and they have two children. His wife's name is Erin, and she has a master's degree in education teaching at the high-school level. It is a joy to have her in the family. They live about two hours from us so visiting them is no problem, but at the same time we are not in one another's backyard.

Sarah also was involved with soccer at a young age, competing in the Burlington Soccer Club, Burlington High School soccer, and a sixteen and over traveling club team. They took first place in their club team, and Sarah earned first team all-county and first team all-conference in high school. She was awarded four varsity letters. She was a coach in the Burlington Soccer Club and was also offered a full scholarship at the college level to play soccer. She turned that down and was then awarded a full scholarship through SBC Communication, beating out forty two hundred people for two hundred scholarships.

She earned a bachelor's of psychology and a master's of psychology, majoring in school counseling. When she walked into her first job, she met a young man named Mike, and they later stated at that moment they knew they would marry each other. It took four years for that to work out, but it finally happened. They are a perfect match, and they balance each other perfectly. He was a teacher at the time but has since received a master's degree in school business administration and is working in that field now. They just bought a house and are expecting their first child. I could not have asked for better spouses for my children or parents for my grandchildren. It's amazing how a man who is intimidated by people with higher education has so many in his family.

Chapter 25

For years we went to Deb's parents' house on Christmas Eve. It was something Deb and the kids looked forward to. I enjoyed it for a while until the booze started to become more and more of the focal point. At holidays or family functions, I always took a second car so I could leave any time I started to feel closed in. We told them it was because I might be called to work or I was going to a meeting later but in fact it was an escape for me when it became too chaotic. I could take being around the drinking for just so long, and then I had to leave, and it's still that way today.

There were times when I scheduled myself to work weekends or holidays just so I didn't have to go. You have to do what you have to do to maintain sobriety. Sobriety comes first in my life, for if I don't have that I surely won't have anything else. I would always be home for Christmas, but any other holiday was open to work. I turned into a workaholic after we finished the house and stayed that way until I retired. Being a workaholic was also a way of dealing with the other illness I had and didn't know about. It provided enough money for Deb and the kids to live a life I had only dreamed of when I was growing up. We were not rich, but I don't believe we lacked for anything and would have been considered upper middle income.

Deb and the kids could spend as much time as they wanted at her folks. The kids enjoyed being with their cousins, and they all liked playing in the store when it was closed. I believe her family was relieved when I left or didn't show. I would usually say something sooner or later that would irritate someone. There were times when Deb and the kids didn't get invited to social events at her folks' house because either they didn't want to take the chance of me coming or they knew Deb would not approve of what was going on. The kids knew this also and mentioned it off and on while growing up. We were headed in different directions is what it amounted to. There are other things I could say, but that's Deb's story.

I received a phone call one morning just before I left for work from my sister. I was expecting her to tell me the old man had died since he had been in and out of the hospital for months. Instead she said our brother Butch had died in his sleep. That was a shock even though I knew he was not in good health, but I didn't think he was that serious. He died of heart failure during the night. As soon as I hung up, I went upstairs to tell Deb and then called my boss, asking for death in the family leave. I knew there was a meeting at nine thirty that morning so I went to that. There would have been a time when I would have gone to the bar, staying drunk during and after the funeral. On the day of the funeral, I helped carry him to the chapel but was glad when a young fellow pushed me out of the way when we started to carry him to the grave site. He weighed almost four hundred pounds, and I am getting too old. Often in life there are things you can't fix, and Butch's health problems were one of them.

The term *child abuse* is often used by the news media as a way to get what they want to see happen politically. It has gotten to a point in our society where parents are afraid to discipline their children for fear of retaliation from the authorities. I saw a father in Burlington, Wisconsin tell his daughter to get into their van repeatedly, but she kept back talking him. This went on until he had the grocery bags put away, and then with one movement, he took hold of her arm, and using his foot to guide her, he put her in the van.

About that time a guy came running across the parking lot screaming child abuse. The dad told the guy in no uncertain terms that this was his daughter and he would discipline her the way he saw fit and for him to stay out of it. When the guy doing the screaming saw that he wasn't going to get any help he backed off quickly. Most cowards do. I was standing less than ten feet from where this happened, and if I had thought for one minute that he had abused his daughter, I would have been having words with him myself. But what he did was use his foot to guide her into the van; he did not kick or hurt that child in any way. She did not cry out or start crying as she sat there. It was a good lesson for her, and it was the father's right as her dad to teach her to listen and act according to what he wanted her to do. Too often the child thinks that they are the one in charge.

I am not saying there is no child abuse out there. I have not only experienced it on a personal level, but God knows I've seen enough of it over the years and witnessed the end results when I go into jails, prisons, and rehabilitation centers. Society has too long put the label of child abuse on every type of discipline parent's use with their children. That is one of the main reasons we have the problems we have with kids today, which is no respect for their elders, their parents or life. If there is no discipline in one's life, there will only be chaos.

Fathers have failed to be fathers, thinking they are fathers because they can biologically help make a child. There is far more to being a father than just providing sperm. Now it is to the point where mothers don't want to be mothers after they have a baby. They would rather leave the baby in a trash dump or try to flush it down a toilet. Believe me when I say that we as a society have caused and are responsible for this mess we now find ourselves in. How many times have I heard in jails and prisons that if they could only get out, they would be home every night with their children? I called one guy on it, and he had to admit that if he was on the street at that moment he would be looking to get high instead of being home with his kids. We need to get honest with ourselves.

I believe Deb and the kids know I love them more than life itself. Even though I disappear into my own little world or head downstairs to be by myself, they know. Sarah told her mom last summer when I didn't go fishing with them that I was in my downtime mode. I believe they love me, but there are times they would just as soon not have me around. I am not saying that as something bad, but that is how I see it. Besides, everyone is busy living their lives, and that is how it should be. I am not the easiest person to be around for any length of time. It is not the life I want; it is just the way it is. This stems from what happened just before and after I retired when my world fell in on me.

After I retired, we moved from Burlington to be in the middle of where the kids lived. I thought I would handle the move better than Deb, but my whole world came crashing down on me. I have a friend who served in the Seal Teams for thirteen years, and he told me when I retired that PTSD was going to whip up on me like it never had before. I told him he was nuts. I had dealt with that at the meetings and didn't see any problem coming from that. This was the same guy who always referred to me as the army puke. Anyway, a year and a half later, I called him to tell him he had been right. All he said was, "Once an army puke; always an army puke," and then he hung up. This is the same guy who told me recently that I should embrace my insanity. You have to love those navy seals.

When I went to have my records sent to the Tomah Veterans Administration, at Toma Wisconsin, they had me meet with a nurse practitioner who began to ask me questions. Two of the answers must have gotten their attention because there was a message on my answering machine when I got home wanting me back at the hospital right away. One question was when I had last thought of killing someone, and I told her earlier that week. The other question was when was the last time I had thought of killing myself and I told her that morning. They took these two answers very seriously and wanted me to talk with someone. I didn't want anything to do with the VA other than medical because I didn't trust them and didn't want to be bothered by them. They didn't want anything to do with us when we came back from 'Nam so why should I trust them now? So out the door I went, and I found out later they had tried to stop me before I made it to the door.

There is a nurse practitioner named Debra Frazer who goes to our church and works as a triage nurse for mental health at the VA. For over a year she kept telling me to come and see her because she knew I had a problem, but I kept blowing her off. All during this time there was not a day when I didn't think of blowing my brains out. I was totally alone, helpless, and without hope. I knew I was the scum of the earth and they should either lock me up or I would take matters in to my own hands. The light had not only gone out at the end of the tunnel, but they had removed all the equipment for the light.

I sunk deeper and deeper into PTSD and didn't know I was going there. I couldn't drink so that was not an option. Instead I went to a lot of meetings because I knew I was safe there. Just like in the beginning, I knew I would be safe for that hour or so. Even though they didn't understand what I was going through, there was acceptance.

My wife didn't understand because in her mind the Vietnam War was forty some years ago and I should be over it and she didn't want to hear about it. She didn't believe there was anything wrong with me. I thought I was finally going insane and there wasn't a damn thing I could do about it so the most logical thing to do was blow my brains out. An alcoholic or combat veteran will find a solution to a problem; it just might not be the one society is willing to accept. I would start crying for no reason and get the shakes, with my mind spinning out of control, going wherever it wanted to. I felt like there was no purpose or reason for life. I felt there was no beginning or end—that it was just there and I was trapped in it. Remember, this all happened after I had been sober and trusting Jesus for over thirty years.

I was sitting downstairs surfing the channels when a program came on television about PTSD. They were having a panel discussion with some of the guys who had served in Iraq. One of the guys said something about security checks during the middle of the night and before going to sleep. That struck a nerve because I had been doing it for forty years. After that statement got my attention, I listened closer to what they were saying, and like they say, it is one veteran helping another veteran and I finally accepted the fact I needed help. There is no better example of God intervening in someone's life than this. I called Deb Frazer at the VA, telling her what I had just heard and that I thought I should come in and see someone. She made all the appointments for me, and over the course of the last couple of years, I was finally able to enjoy Christmas this year with the family—maybe not to the degree that most people do but a lot more than I used to.

I took the following disorders from the book *Veterans' and Families' Guide to Recovering from PTSD* written by Stephanie Laite Lanham. I wrote next to them how they have affected me over the course of forty-some years. This is a very helpful book, and I recommend it to any combat veteran.

Anger: I don't consider what I went through over the years to be anger but rage. I would go from nothing to red-hot rage in a heartbeat. I came home from 'Nam full of rage, and it stayed there for the next twenty-some years. There was physical abuse in my first marriage and a whole lot of verbal abuse. The marriage lasted five years. There was constant drinking during this time. After the marriage, I finally got sober at twenty-nine years old and remarried at thirty. My wife told me at the end of sixteen years that I had a year to get rid of what she referred to as my anger or she was taking the kids and leaving. It took nine months of counseling before I could start to deal with it. I don't have the rage, but I can still get extremely angry at times. The only difference is I let it go quicker than I used to. I have found that since I retired the anger is turned inward more.

Anxiety/Hyperarousal: I have had anxiety problems ever since 'Nam. They seem to be getting worse the older I get. There are times when I feel like I could crawl out of my skin. There could be nothing wrong, but in my head the whole world is coming to an end. My body is like a banjo where the strings have been over tightened. I think this is one of the reasons I was never able to sleep well. I would wake up in the middle of the night over the slightest noise and then lay there for the next two hours thinking about horrible things that never happen.

Chronic Pain: I have suffered from this for over forty years. I was in my early thirties when I went into the hospital to try to find out why I hurt so much. After four days in the hospital, the doctors said that physically there was nothing wrong with me. But over the years my bones have felt like they are blowing up. My muscles and joints ache, and I am constantly tired. There were times when I was working when I would have to pull my truck over, taking a power nap for five minutes or so. This could be a couple times a day. I still suffer from this. They say these are the golden years, and if that is the case then I would rather be in the dark ages.

Crisis: I find it harder to deal with situations that used to be no big deal. They seem harder to comprehend and fix. It gets frustrating.

Denial: I was told years ago I had PTSD from other vets who had it. A navy seal friend told me I was going to have a rough time after I retired, and I told him he was nuts. I thought I had dealt with all this through the meetings over the last thirty-some years. I did not realize it is a different type of situation. There are still days when I think that it is crap and I just need to move on, but the only problem is I don't know how to do that or what I am moving on from.

Depression: This is a bad one for me. I have suffered with it ever since 'Nam and have been on and off medication for over forty years. I can remember telling my wife one night that the light went off at the end of the tunnel. There have been long periods of depression for me. Then there is all the thoughts that go with it that drag you into the ever-bigger hole of darkness. If it had not been for the meetings, I know I would not have made it this far. And when it comes on me, my first thought is to withdraw into my safe place. This has robbed me of the closeness I see other men having with their families. I feel distant and withdrawn from them, and it sucks.

Flashbacks: I think of 'Nam if I hear a chopper or smell diesel fumes. Loud noises also take me back there. We were up at a lake this past summer, and someone was setting off firecrackers. They must have been big ones because they vibrated around the lake. After about four of them, my skin began to crawl, and I became agitated and uptight. With each one that went off, I wanted to scream. My whole body reacted in a way that it hadn't in a long time. I started to breathe faster, wanting to run, but there was nowhere to go.

Guilt: I felt like a man without a country when I came back. I felt guilty for leaving my buddies over there and found myself staying away from talk of 'Nam. Twice I was asked if I killed someone over there, and both times I felt sick to my stomach and somehow like I had been violated. I constantly feel guilty even though I might not have done anything.

Isolation: I am finding myself doing this more and more as I get older. I used to be very active with things but not anymore. I have to force myself to get involved. The wife has to talk me into vacations and going anywhere. There is a part of me that does not want to isolate, but then the other part does. I never know which side is going to win. The more I isolate myself, the more alone I feel.

Loneliness: I can be in a room of one hundred people and feel all alone. It helps if another veteran or a recovering drunk is there. Then I feel like I have someone to relate to, but then there are times when this does not work. The people can be very friendly, but I still feel alone. There are times when I feel that even God has deserted me, but I know that is a lie.

Low Self-Esteem: I have had this for a very long time. Don't feel like I measure up to other people. This can include veterans and even members of my own family. Both of my children have graduate degrees, and at times I feel like the dumbest man in the world. I get very insecure around people who I feel are a success in the world. This even carried over into my work. Even though I was very good at what I did, I always felt like the other workers knew more or were better than I was.

Obsessions: I have a problem with counting corners and the sides of straight lines on objects. Have been doing this for over twenty years that I can remember. And when I am caught up in this, I miss what is going on around me.

Paranoia/Hypervigilance: This has bothered me since 'Nam. I always look for a quick way out of any place I am in. I will study the people around me to see who I think will be the most likely to start something or be a threat, I like having my back against something and even looking for something to break a window with if I have to get out fast. I don't like my windows left open at night and will check the doors several times before I go to bed. I even lock the door to downstairs when I go to bed. If the wife is not there, I will load up the shotgun and leave it handy. I have thought about where rounds would hit the house if someone went by and shot into it. I don't like to answer the door if I don't know who is on the other side. I don't trust strangers or sometimes people I know.

Passive-Aggressive Behavior: Have done this to keep people at arm's length. I've always said that if they think you are crazier than them they will leave you alone.

Phobia: I don't like being around people with guns or knives. This includes police and especially hunters. My three-year-old granddaughter was over the other weekend, and someone got her screaming as they played with her. The more she screamed, the more my skin crawled and my nerves went crazy. By the time they stopped, I was a complete wreck inside. My whole body was wound as tight as a drum. I can't take loud, sharp noises because they set my whole system off.

Sleep Disorders: I have slept on the edge, never getting to that deep sleep I need since, I came back from 'Nam. Sleeping like that means I wake up to every noise and then lay awake for the next couple hours with my mind racing. For years I dreaded going to bed as I knew that it was going to be a very long lonely night. I would wake up

in the morning more tired than when I went to
bed. And this was night after night. The doctor
has me on something to sleep now, and the first
night I took it I thought to myself, *So this is what
a good night's sleep is like.* I still have two or three
flashback dreams a year. During the last one I woke
up with a handful of my wife's hair, getting ready
to rip it out. In the dream I was wrestling with a VC
for his rifle.

Substance Abuse: I drank heavily after I got home
from 'Nam. At twenty-nine I found the meetings
and have been sober ever since.

Suicidal Thoughts or Ideation: I have often
thought of suicide over the years. I am surprised
when people tell me they never have.

As I sat down to write that last section, my hands and
mind were shaking so bad it was hard to focus on what I
was putting down.

Deb unknown to me made hotel reservations at Green
Bay, Wisconsin, for LZ Lambeau held in May 2010. I didn't
want to go because I thought it was a bunch of stupid
politicians trying to drum up votes about how they are
now supporting the Vietnam veteran. But since she made
the arrangements, I went. Other than marrying me and
having our two children, this was the best present she ever
gave me, and I will be forever grateful to her.

The Green Bay Packers let the veterans use the
stadium, and it was veterans putting it on. There were
approximately twenty-four thousand 'Nam veterans there
that weekend who thought the same way I did. The final

piece had been put back in me. I was once again home with my brothers in arms. Just writing that sentence brings tears to my eyes. I was not alone anymore in how I thought or how I reacted to life. Is the PTSD gone? No, and it never will be, but at least I can live with it a little better.

It took LZ Lambeau to break the wall I put around my heart those many years ago when I walked out of Rodeitcher's bar. I am no longer ashamed of being a Vietnam combat veteran and have started to accept what I have gone through for my country even though at the time I was labeled for it. I have been privileged to walk with men of valor and honor. They laid their lives on the line for their fellow man and their country. They know better than anyone what the taste of freedom is because they fought the battles for it, with many dying in those battles. There was a sergeant major who wrote an article, and in it he stated, "When we join the military we give our government a blank check to do with us what they will and that includes the forfeiture of our lives if that is what's called for." I wish I could remember the man's name to give him full credit because no one has ever said it better.

There is an invocation that was spoken by Col. Jack Hayes, a Texas Ranger in the Mexican War:

> Lord, we are about to join battle with vastly superior numbers of enemy, and heavenly Father, we would like you to be on our side and help us, but if you can't do it, for Christ's sake don't go over to them but lie low and keep dark, and you'll see the damndest fight you ever saw in all your born days.
>
> Amen

An older woman both in sobriety and years said it well the other night when she told a newcomer to listen to what I said because there was wisdom in my words when I spoke about alcoholism and how to stay sober, but it also came with the same amount of insanity. You have to love the honesty.

I was at a meeting at a secure rehabilitation facility the other night, and we were discussing our lives as we grew up. This man said he left home when he was a freshman in high school because he could not take the beatings any more. Every time his dad got drunk he caught the abuse, both verbal and physical, because he was the oldest and that made him the punching bag. When the school found out they asked the father what he was going to do about his drinking. He told them he was not giving up his booze for anyone, and that included his wife and kids. Years later as his dad lay dying he went back to try to mend the relationship before his dad passed on. Before he died, his grown children were around the bed and asked him if there was anything they could get him. His reply was alcohol because he heard there was no alcohol in heaven. They gave him a little whiskey, and shortly after he became comatose, dying a few days later. It is easy to understand because that is what alcoholism does.

People want to think that mankind has evolved to this majestic level—that some are more evolved than others and so on and so on. Take off the blinders and look around at what is happening in this world. If we have become so intellectually elite then why are we running headlong toward the abyss of oblivion? Why is there so much hatred, killing, rape, stealing (legal and illegal), children whose parents have left, drug and alcohol addictions, politicians who are more concerned about themselves than their constituents, and on and on it goes? If you want to find common sense in this world I urge you not to go to any of the world capitols because there is none there.

Man has not changed since the beginning of time. He is just more cunning in how he goes about things. Let's list some of our finer qualities: pride, anger, lust, hatred, bigotry, and envy, with the list going on and on. Most people blame God even though they don't believe he exists when the reality is that God has given man freedom to do what he wants, so whose fault is it really? We told God to leave our schools, our government, and even some of our churches have said they will no longer follow all of his teachings because Jesus surely could not have meant this or that. Then we wonder why he is not there when trouble comes. We are the ones who told him to leave. Are there good people out there? Most certainly, but I believe there are more bad than good or could it be just the life I lived? Even bad people can do good things, but that doesn't make them good.

I wrote this book for people like me to let them know there is hope. I know where they are because I walked it, lived it, and breathed it. Book knowledge is far from me, but I have been blessed in learning to live life on life's terms and to survive when others have died. God has done for me what I couldn't do for myself, which was get me sober, keep me sober, and stop me from killing myself or someone else along the way.

I am not an easy person to be around because I'm strong willed and very opinionated. People spend their whole lives acquiring stuff only to realize in the end (if they are lucky) it is all meaningless. The one with the most toys does not win; it just means that person's family has a lot of stuff to get rid of when they die. The most-treasured morsel of knowledge I have acquired through the hard knocks of life is to know that God exist and loves me. How do I know this? There were times when I should have died, times when I should have been taken prisoner, and more times than I can recount when my very emotional wellbeing was in question. But I am here, I am somewhat sane, and I am alive to tell you about it.

I asked God to show me things over the years. I asked him for ten years what happened to Tammy Jo Hanley and where she was. Over the course of time I talked to many people, and eventually one of them told me she had died in California in 2001. The remarkable part was I didn't ask this person anything about Tammy. I never had contact with this person before or since. She was placed there to give me the answer and then was gone.

About a month ago while I was in Midland, Michigan, talking to Don, my brother-in-law, I asked how to find which cemetery Tammy would be buried in. He got on his computer and within five minutes told me she was buried less than two miles from where we were sitting. I went to the cemetery and walked through it until I found her gravesite. Another example of prayer answered.

When I joined the military I wanted to go to the combat engineers but ended up in the signal corps. This also was a God thing because I retired from AT&T forty-three years later, enjoying every minute of it. And when people said I would end up in prison God took that statement, making it happen for His glory. Over the years I have visited numerous prisons, and whenever it came time to leave, they let me walk out. Now that's a God thing.

Years ago Josh was sick for about a week, and as I was walking across a field talking to God about it, God showed up. I started to fall to my knees because I had no strength in my legs, but he held me up, saying, "I will heal the child in my time." You can recognize God's voice for it is sweet, soft and gentle, and He is direct and to the point. It is easy to see God's work in hindsight but the thing is to recognize him working in the moment or trusting him for the future. When I am in the middle of chaos and my life seemingly hangs on the edge, I need to look for God because he is always there. It is not the outcome God is concerned about for he already knows that but how I am going to go through the chaos. Do I turn to him, or do I curse him for allowing whatever it is in my life? I have done both.

I asked God a number of years back why he cursed me with these bodily cravings. Everything my body or mind likes it wants more and more of, even if it takes me to the point of death. He told me it was not a curse from him but something I had chosen years before through the path in life I took. He could not get me out of it until I asked him to, and that is when he turned it into my greatest blessing. Because of what I have been through there are people I can reach and touch for him that others can't and they will relate because I have been there.

I'm allowed to go to jails, prisons, and rehabilitation facilities and deal with broken people—people addicted to porn, booze, drugs, and everything under the sun. I offer what I have found to break the chains that hold them to their addiction. People blame God for everything that happens to them, but life's problems are because of choices we made somewhere along the road of life or because someone else has made a decision and because of that we get sucked in, such as wars, muggings, rapes, killings, etc. It is not the gun or bomb that does the killing but someone who is trying to impose his or her will on someone else. And it seems like there are more and more people and nations that want to impose their will upon others. Here is a jewel I was given that speaks volumes.

Treasures in Prison Cells
Bill Yount

It was late at night and I was tired . . . but about midnight God spoke to me in my spirit asking me a question.

"Bill, where on earth does man keep his most priceless treasure and valuables? I said "Lord usually these treasures like gold, silver, diamonds and precious jewels are kept locked up somewhere out of sight, usually with guards and security to keep them under lock and key.

God spoke. "Like man, my most valuable treasures on earth are also locked up." Then I saw Jesus standing in front of seemingly thousands of prisons and jails. The Lord said, "They have almost been destroyed by the enemy, but these souls have the greatest potential to be used, and to bring forth glory to my name. Tell my people; I am going this hour to the prisons to activate the gifts and callings that lie dormant in these lives that were given before the foundation of the earth. Out from these walls will come forth a spiritual army that will have power to literally kick down the gates of hades and overcome satanic powers that are holding many of my people bound in my own House.

"Tell my people that great treasure is behind these walls, in these forgotten vessels. My people must come forth and touch these lives for a mighty anointing will be unleashed upon them for future victory in my kingdom, they must be restored.

Then I saw the Lord step up to the doors with a key. One key fit every lock and the gates began to open. Then I heard and saw great explosions that sounded like dynamite going off behind the walls. It sounded like all out spiritual warfare. Jesus turned and said, "Tell my people to go in now and pick up the spoil and rescue them." Jesus then began walking in and touching inmates who were thronging him. Many being touched instantly began to have a golden glow come over them. God spoke to me, "There's the gold!" Others had a silver glow around them. God said, "There's the silver!"

Like slow motion they began to grow into what appeared to be giant knights, armed warriors. They had on the armor of God and every piece was solid and pure gold. Even golden shields! When I saw the golden shields, I heard God say to these warriors, "Now go and take what Satan has taught you and use it against him. Go an pull down the strongholds coming against my church" The spiritual giants then started stepping over the prison walls with no one to resist then and they went immediately to the very front line of battle with the enemy, I saw them walk right past the church, big name ministers who were known for their power with God were surpassed by the giant warriors like David going after Goliath! They crossed the enemy's line and started delivering many of God's people from the clutches of Satan while demons trembled and fled out of sight at their presence. No one, not even the church seemed to know who these spiritual giants were or where they came from. They were restored to God's House and there was great rejoicing. I also saw silver, precious treasures, and vessels being brought in. Beneath the gold and silver were the people that nobody knew: Rejects of society, street people, the outcasts, the poor and the despised. These were the treasures that were missing from His House.

In closing The Lord said, "If my people want to know where they are Needed, tell them they are needed in the streets, the hospitals, the missions and prisons. When they come there they will find me and the next move of my Spirit and they will be judged by my word in (Matt. 25:42-43).

Clark, a buddy of mine, said it well in that he knows two and two are four and it drives him nuts. That makes sense to me. The only time I am different from other people is when I am drinking or in a dry drunk. That is when all the alcohol thought processes are in full gear except I have had no actual booze. But if I stay there long enough, I will eventually pick up and use. Other than that, I am just as sane as the rest of the world. Now that is scary! How do I keep from falling into this state of mind? I go to meetings and try to improve my conscious contact with God on a daily and sometimes moment-by-moment basis.

The human mind is extremely powerful; tricking people into believing they are well and once again can handle that which was once killing them. I know this because I have seen it over and over. I have been to a great many funerals of people who went back to booze and drugs, thinking they could handle just one. I have a friend named Denny who was on Librium for over thirty years and had not taken a drop of alcohol for well over thirty-five years. One morning he woke up and decided he no longer needed his medication and stopped taking it. He almost died while the doctors were trying to get him regulated again. Our thought process can be our worst enemy.

One of the words coming out of the counseling field when I got sober by God's grace was *feelings*. How do you feel about this and that? They wanted everyone to get in touch with their feelings and inner child. An old-timer told me he didn't give a damn how I felt; it was time to grow up. He knew I had a problem, and I was it. He never allowed me do the blame game, and it was just too damn bad if my childhood sucked. He told me I had three outcomes if I refused to stop drinking: commitment to an insane asylum, life in prison, or death.

People come out of treatment today thinking they have all the answers because someone gave them a coin saying they graduated from their program. They bring this coin and what they perceive the counselors told them back to the meetings and have been doing it for years. That is why the success rate has gone from 75 percent to around 5 percent. I am not saying treatment centers are bad, for they aren't, but they have to be used in conjunction with and not as a substitute for meetings.

In my opinion the best counselors are the ones who have been there. I have known a few over the years who were not alcoholics and they were excellent, but this was after they had been in the counseling field for some time. Once again book knowledge is just that. You have to have your hands in it for a while to become effective. I don't believe the only way to get off booze and drug's is at meetings. Your chances are better if you go to them, but I know of people who woke up one morning and never touched the stuff again. My brother stopped his drinking by using the church and intense counseling over a period of time.

The one thing that all the successful ones do, though, is that they clean up their past and don't go back to it. They also establish a relationship with God. Some people quit drinking but never do anything else, living out the rest of their lives hating everyone and everything until a miserable death takes them. There was a song called "Daddy's Hands" that drove me nuts. It talked about how they were so loving and caring. I couldn't relate to that and still can't. I took it to God, and he said, "Phil, I am your spiritual Father, and I am the one who made you even though I used your earthly father to do it. Look to me and no one else, for I am the Father you seek."

Another very important thing I do to stay sober is give it back. When you first start going to meetings, the giving back is to other alcoholics, but as you get further into sobriety, you recognize that it is also to society. I used and abused people when I drank and did drugs, and why wouldn't I? I thought I was the center of the universe. People were there for me to use as I wanted to, whether it was for money, sex, power, amusement, or whatever.

The non-alcoholics think the active alcoholic and drug addict are bottom feeders in how they live life, but are they any different? I don't think so. I have seen them over the years doing the exact same things the drunk does, only they say it is for the advancement of one thing or another. Usually that advancement has something to do with them climbing whatever ladder of life they happen to be on. They are just as blinded by their own variety of greed and selfishness as the alcoholic.

I found out later that a number of people I grew up with endured some of the same things I have as far as divorced parents, their own divorces, fighting, rebellion, attempted suicides, going to jail and prison. I went to a meeting in Freeland, Michigan, about twenty years ago, and sitting across from me was a man who was about my age. It turned out that he was a friend of mine from the old neighborhood and had been sober for a number of years. The last time I had seen him he was passed out at Rodietcher's bar, and now here he was sober.

One of the saddest things that can happen to people is for them to think they have arrived, not having to do anything else for themselves or for mankind. I have found that the rich give a lot of money to charities, but few of them stand on the soup line giving out the food. It was good enough to give the money, making them feel better about themselves. Let the lower level be the servers of the food. There are exceptions but not many.

I give back because it is what God wants me to do. And from giving I get self-worth and a feeling that at long last I am doing what I was born for. Do I always want to go to meetings or give back? No, but I have come to realize over the years that the times I don't want to but do are the times I am most blessed. It's like God had something special he wanted to give me or have me hear during those times. Most of the people I give back to are ones society would rather forget about. That is why they are in prisons and institutions. Should they be there? Yes they should because of the crimes they have committed. Some of them will never see the light of freedom again. Is that justice? Yes it is, for society needs to be protected from them. But just because they are locked up is no reason to forget them. Even the most vicious animal deserves kindness of some form. Should a human deserve any different?

But for God's grace that's me in the prison cell, and I need to remember it. Anyone is capable of doing the most heinous act at any given moment, and if we think we wouldn't, we are only fooling ourselves. The things I have said so far may not sit well with some, but if that is the case maybe God is telling you there are areas of your life you need to look at.

Is the God of the Bible at our meetings? I would say yes for I have watched people saved and lives changed because of what takes place at the meetings. It also says in Scripture that God is everywhere (Ps. 139:7-12 NKJV). Are there other gods at our meetings? Again the answer is yes for there are those who believe in other gods and those who believe in no god. Are these meetings any different from what goes on in life and churches everywhere? The answer is no.

There are religious leaders who say our meetings are satanic or occult because the terminology of God as you understand him is used. Is it any different than their meetings in that people coming through their doors are seeking a God they don't understand? And who does it fall upon to teach them? Our meetings are not to get people saved (even though some are); they are to get a person sober long enough to make a sane choice. Before sobriety I was not able to choose. And the choice I had to make was do I want to serve Jesus Christ or don't I? Even if at the end they choose to serve another god or no god, at least they are sober and not beating or molesting their family, friends, and society. They are bringing their paychecks home, staying out of jail and prison, and becoming contributing members of society.

The Devil is sitting in the front pew of every denominational and nondenominational church throughout the United States. Not all people who say they are Christians are. We have so-called believers within churches who have wandered so far from the truth of the Bible that they would no longer be considered Christian. But in these backslidden denominations God has saved a remnant for himself. It is easy to point your finger at other churches, for then you don't have to look at yourself. It is not about denominations or non-denominations but about a relationship between yourself and God through his Son, Jesus. The Bible has no gray areas in it and speaks just as loudly to the saved, the so-called saved, and the lost. I heard a man say the other day that the Bible has contradictions in it, and he used the gospels as an example. This man apparently doesn't know the flow of the gospels or he would not have said that. But people are people. Everyone wants to be an authority on something.

So what do I know? I have come to the realization that I don't have the answers and that is okay, for at one time I thought I did. I have a lot of experiences I can share with people, but that is all I have. Like Solomon said, "Vanity of vanities, says the Preacher; Vanity of vanities, all is vanity" (Eccles.1:2 NKJV) There are times when Solomon used the word vanity and it meant "vapor," which in this statement it does. Life is but a vapor, so fleeting and so short when compared to eternity.

We think when we are young that life goes on forever just as it is, but in truth, all things are constantly changing. Ask an old person how long ago they were young, and they will tell you yesterday. There will be good times and bad times, and they are both a gift. The good times are a blessing from God and the bad times are when God allows something into our lives as a teaching moment. When your world is crashing down around you, look for God in the middle of the storm. Investigate what God wants to teach you in the midst of the turmoil.

It has been said over the centuries that God will never give you more than you can handle. I believe that statement is misunderstood. God will always give you more than you can handle because that is one of the ways he draws you to him. We constantly try to figure out life, but in the end we are driven to our knees, asking God for the solution. God will always give us a way of escape (1 Cor. 10:12-13 NKJV).

God states in his instruction book that anyone who believes God does not exist is a fool (Ps. 53:1 NKJV). I was a fool for many years, and I paid a heavy price. There are people who don't believe God exist because they assume they are in charge of their destiny, and that is why I was a fool. I believed in God, but I also thought I could direct my destiny to what I wanted it to be. I believe I can proceed in a general direction but the outcome will always be God's.

A sense of achievement is good, but pride draws you away from the one who gave you the knowledge needed to accomplish the task set before you.

Do you wear your Christianity as a badge of honor or humbly as one saved from the executioner? I have done both, but it always has been when I wore it humbly that I felt the hand of God on me. I don't believe God is honored when his children wave their salvation as a flag of triumph. Yes we are saved but only through what Christ did and not through anything of ourselves.

What I wrote is what I believe God wanted me to. Deb says I live too much in the past and that is why I rarely enjoy today. Maybe she is right, but if she is, that makes me one sick puppy. Why would anyone want to relive what I have been through? But as I help people, there are bits and pieces that come up as I share my story. Some say I should put it behind me and move on.

I know I don't interact well with a great deal of people. Sometimes it concerns me, but most of the time it doesn't. Deb expresses she is weary of being asked how she has put up with me over the years. She is tired of the chaos I bring to the table and would like her remaining years to be peaceful. I have been told by the VA that I have PTSD, but I am working on the issues associated with that. I am a flawed individual, with parts of those flaws always going to be there. I pray daily that the latter part of Deb's life will be better than the first part and peace will reign within her.

It's during the times when Deb wants me to be something I am not that I don't know which way to turn. Deb wants me to be a normal husband (whatever that is), and God wants me to love and feed his sheep. But where

God has placed me is where the chaos is, and there are people who will not go there. That's not bragging but a statement of fact. There are people at the meetings who will not go to some of the places I go to.

Perhaps there is part of me that enjoys the adrenalin rush because I never know what is going to happen. It is not just the dysfunctional family I came from or the alcoholism because you have to throw in PTSD from two tours in Vietnam. There are times when I would like to turn my back on everything and I mean everything and walk away. I would love not having to think about if I am going to get smacked at a meeting because I made people mad by telling them what they didn't want to hear. Or maybe someone gets out of jail or prison that you went eyeball to eyeball with and wants to have a chat with you.

I remember being on my knees in front of that couch over thirty-seven years ago, crying out to God and being shown how he views humanity. Can I turn my back on that vision and walk away? I would not be able to live with myself if I did. I don't believe I live in the past, but I go there and grab something that can help me reach someone if I have to. Just maybe someday I will be that old man sitting on his front porch drinking a cup of coffee and thanking God for everything he has been given. Is it going to happen tomorrow? No, but it might happen someday. I will be glad when this book is complete because it has taken me to places I had long shied away from and to the edge of a very deep cavern that holds to many forgotten secrets.

I believe God is the same now as he was in the beginning (Heb. 13:8 NKJV). I believe he saves, heals, blesses, and prospers his people. But I do not believe he is an ATM machine for us to go to whenever we want. There are people who believe they are little gods and can use his Word to petition from God anything they want, and he has to do it for them. They believe this by taking his Word out of context. But in the same breath they would say I am the one doing it. The difficulty with their thought progression is they forget that God is the potter and we are the clay (Rom. 9:18-21 NKJV).

Permit me to share an illustration of why alcoholics and drug addicts have a hard time with established religion. First of all, many of them come from religious backgrounds, having grown up in the church. Over the years they have seen what different religions, denominations, and non-denominations have done against one another all in the name of God—this one believing they are right and that one assuming they are right with some thinking they have a new revelation from God.

Deb and I were recently told that we didn't comprehend certain doctrines of the Bible because we weren't matured enough to grasp God's Word even though we have taught and been in Bible studies for more than thirty years in different denominations. The person who told us this adheres to the prosperity or the name it and claim it gospel, which we do not believe in. The more we tried to discuss it with the individual, the more defensive they became.

Some people will believe anything if they think they are going to get something out of it. God calls it having itching ears (2 Tim. 4:3-5 NKJV). Ten years ago I would have applied God's Word and torn holes in the so-called revelations of this theology, and even though I had a heated discussion, it just wasn't worth it.

After I stopped drinking and drugging by God's grace, I started to listen to the prosperity gospel crowd on television. They were just starting out. The more you give, the more you get is the way they described it. Do I believe you can't out-give God? Yes I do, but it is not continuously about material things like they would have you believe, and it is not constantly about things on earth (Matt. 6:19-21 NKJV). I was receiving their magazines at the time and read them from cover to cover. I was involved with this faction twenty years before the individual at the Bible study ever heard of it.

One day God told me under no circumstances was I to have anything to do with this movement again. He never gave me a reason, just informed me not to have anything more to do with them. It was during this time that I was continuously on my knees before God since I realized that by being as close to him as I could, I would stay free from alcohol.

According to the individual within the Bible study and some evangelists and preachers on television, the solitary basis of someone being sick, poor, or in need is because they lack the faith it takes to acquire what they desire from God. They lack the maturity needed to understand the true significance of what the Scriptures say.

I have witnessed countless people over the years that died long, slow, horrible deaths from illnesses, these were devoted Christians. They did everything the "name it and claim it" movement conveys you have to do. They spent a great deal of their time in prayer and supplication, giving money to the extent that some had nothing left. They had the elders of the church anoint them with oil, lay hands on them, and pray for healing. Some went to the big-name faith healers time and time again. They were not slackers of the faith because every one of them deep within their hearts believed they would be healed or granted what they prayed for.

Some of these brothers and sisters were in the prosperity movement and some were not, but the thing they had in common is that most suffered and died. Were some given what they petitioned God for? The answer would be yes but not all. So the thing I would ask is, were all these people's faith weak? Didn't they have enough of God's Spirit to be healed? A dear friend of mine had cancer, which she battled for four years, and then it had its way with her. At the end she told Deb she no longer knew whether to pray for healing or for God to take her home. At one time she told us she knew without a doubt that God had completely healed her.

It is effortless to convey to others what they have to do when it doesn't affect you. By bad mouthing (and that's what it is) somebody else's relationship with Jesus, they puff themselves up. A number of these same people take medications for ailments they have suffered from for years. Or perhaps a member of their family has a terrible affliction but all the praying, laying on of hands, and anointing with oil have not brought forth a healing. The first thing they say is that they keep on believing for whatever they're praying for. Good; that is what God tells us to do, but the final outcome belongs to God and not to us (1 Thess. 5:17-18 NKJV).

Furthermore I have wondered why the preachers on television always seem to need more and more money, with some of them telling you the exact amount to send and how often you should send it. They need your money to build theme parks and then want you to buy a condo using the rationale that you can use it anytime you want. Isn't that called selling time shares? Or else they frighten you with their preaching that the world is coming to an end. But you will be able to survive if you purchase what they are selling. What's sad is that people are buying into it by the droves. What about God will provide?

And then you have your faith healers, which I have often wondered about. If they are so good at healing people then why are they still doing it thirty years later, and why are the hospitals still full? I sat watching television last night, and two guys were saying how God had just told them he was healing people in the television audience. They covered it all in that some of the people being healed had ear problems, neck problems, cancer and stomach problems etc.

I heard a preacher on television make the statement that God could do nothing unless we first tell him to (Ps. 33:6-15). He is not the only one I have heard make such a statement. Where in Scripture does it say that God answers to us? Most of these so-called mighty individuals of God have no gray hair even though they are well past forty years old (could it have come from a box?) and a few of them have obviously had some tucks here and there. I don't remember any of the apostles being rich, but according to this movement's way of interpreting Scripture, none of the apostles would have been considered mature enough or had enough faith.

Where in the Bible does it say Christ healed people and then told them they needed to continue with the same amount of faith or they would lose their healing? These preachers say Christians should not be poor. I would rather be poor in worldly goods and rich in spiritual matters any day of the week. Whenever God's Spirit worked through Jesus, it was always for the benefit of someone and the glory went to God the Father. Jesus stated he did not have a place to lay his head (Matt. 8:19-20 NKJV). We should be ministering to the poor, the widows, and the orphans. The one who wants to be first shall be last (Matt. 19:27-30 NKJV). We are to be a light to the world (Matt. 5:14-16 NKJV). What kind of light will I be to a darkened world if all they see is me wanting more and more stuff?

Should a minister be paid for his work? Most certainly, but when that minister starts to drive luxurious cars, own elaborate houses, and travel all over the world in a private jet then just maybe his pay scale has reached a place it shouldn't be. And if the trustees of their organization are willing to pay the minister that much then possibly they should consider who they really are serving. A good question to ask myself would be: How does my ministry compare to Mother Teresa's? Does my giving resemble hers? I am not a Catholic, but that would be a very good comparison. I believe Jesus wants me to give without expecting anything in return.

In the Beatitudes (Matthew 5:3-12 NKJV) Jesus states:

Blessed are the poor in spirit, for theirs is the kingdom of heaven. Blessed are those who mourn, for they shall be comforted. Blessed are the meek, for they shall inherit the earth. Blessed are those who hunger and thirst for righteousness, for they shall be filled. Blessed are the merciful, for they shall obtain mercy. Blessed are the pure in heart, for they shall see God. Blessed are the peacemakers, for they shall be called sons of God. Blessed are those who are persecuted for righteousness' sake, for theirs is the kingdom of heaven. Blessed are you when they revile and persecute you, and say all kinds of evil against you falsely for My sake. Rejoice and be exceedingly glad, for great is your reward in heaven, for so they persecuted the profits who were before you.

Once we asked Jesus to save us and he became our Lord and Savior (Rom. 10:9-10 NKJV), we were spiritually no longer of this world (John 17:14-16 NKJV). We are passing through on our way home. Why would I want to store up anything where it will rust and decay? I believe I am to use the abilities God gave me and the results are up to God. Jesus Christ of the Bible is the one we should be following, not some movement where people and their interpretation of the Bible are placed on a pedestal.

The first thing Vaughn taught me was to verify and then verify again. Does what they say make sense in relationship to the whole of the Scriptures? Anyone can take Scripture verses, tie them together, and make people believe what they would like them to. Vaughn stated I should pray for spiritual discernment at all times. Without that I would be swung to and fro by every movement that says it has a newer revelation or a greater understanding of God's Word. For me the Bible has no gray areas and does not contradict itself. It is the Word of God that was breathed out for mankind to write down over a long period of time. I must take the whole Bible into consideration when interpreting what I think it is saying to me.

The people at meetings I go to talk about organized religion and not in a flattering way. They have been burned time and again by it and don't trust much of what comes out of it. That is where people like me come in. They have an example before them that declares Christians are not perfect, just forgiven. They have someone who admits he often fails to follow Jesus, and that is why I need him more today than I did yesterday. That it is not about a religion but a relationship. Who among you can say that they have had a perfect relationship with someone their whole life?

I have been at meetings where somebody will try to shout down or embarrass a person who says what his higher power's name is. This happens when the name of Jesus is brought up, and some of them even get mad if you mention God. I ask them how long their God has kept them sober, and usually it isn't very long. I tell them that my God's name is Jesus and what he has done for me over the years. I tell them that I haven't gone back out by His grace since I went to my first meeting thirty-seven years ago. And if their god hasn't done that for them, then maybe they need to check out my God.

I found God in front of a television set with my first wife but found a relationship with him at the meetings. Then I grew in him when I started to go to the place where his instruction book was taught and read. When people ask me to become involved with organized churches, I tell them I don't play well with others, leaving it at that. Then I do what I believe God wants me to do. Pastor Paul of our body of believers said it very well when he said some people get saved within the church but most get saved through the church. In other words within the church is inside the walls of a building whereas through the church is by people who go to the church building and then carry the message outside the walls. I was reminded today at a meeting that Christianity is not a religion, but it is a Christ-centered way of life. The people are the church; they just happen to meet at a building that has the same name.

What is alcoholism? Is it a sin or illness? In my opinion it is both. It starts as a sin, for drunkenness in the Bible is called sin and I agree with that (Eph. 5:18 NKJV). After people journey down the highway of drunkenness long enough, I believe they cross a line that puts them into the realm of alcoholism. It is still a sin to God, but now it has become an illness that takes over our body, mind, and soul. Once you have passed that line, it controls you like nothing ever has and will not let go until you ask for help.

Many people go to their graves thinking they don't have a problem with alcohol or drugs even though their lives are a mess because of it. God is not tolerant of sin, and if I compared where I was when I started drinking to where it took me at the end, I can see how he let me have my way but at the same time loved me enough to make everything I needed available when I became sick and tired of being sick and tired. He allowed me to go the full distance I had to go. And if I had wanted to, I could have taken it to the point of death and beyond. My choice, my life, and my outcome; it was my responsibility. It only became God's when I chose to give it to him and ask for his help and forgiveness. The prayer I use more often than any other is, "Lord, protect me from myself." And yes, there is a book at the meetings I go to that states that we have recovered if we do what we need to. If you don't believe me, read the book.

When I was going through those years of insanity after retirement, I asked at the Bible study, "What is love?" I did not realize how it affected Deb at the time because she thought I was referring to her but I was not. I apologized to her when I found out what she was thinking. I had no idea what it meant because of what I had been going through. For two years I had been living in a state of bitterness, self-hatred, and extreme darkness.

We acquired a cat in early 2008, and Sarah named him Stewie. He was my buddy. He meant more to me than life itself. When he slept with us, he always had his paw touching me. One night I heard a commotion coming from the kitchen. Stewie loved smelling plastic, and on this night he got his head stuck in a plastic bag. I heard him in the kitchen trying to get it off and was just about to get up when I felt his paw on my arm. He knew I would help him, so he came to me. I reached down, taking the bag off his head, and he went on his way. That is the type of relationship and trust we had.

A few months later Stewie started to have trouble breathing. We took him to the veterinarian and at first they thought it was a virus and he would just need some pills. Then the doctor asked if he could give him an x-ray just to make sure. The news was not good. His chest cavity was so full of fluid that they could not see his heart. He had the other doctors at the hospital come and look at the x-rays, and they concluded it was cancer.

Deb and I thought we would be bringing Stewie home but not the way we did. I made the decision to have him put down. Deb went to the lobby because she didn't want to be there when it happened. He saved me so many times from taking my life during those long, dark days, and there was no way I was going to desert him. I was stroking his coat as they gave the shot to relax him. I never took my hand off him because I didn't want him to die alone. I wanted him to feel my presence.

When they came back to give him the final shot, I told the doc that I would rather do Vietnam again than put him down. The doc said he would be back, giving me a little more time with him. I was constantly talking to him and God at the same time. I was mad that this was happening to Stewie and wanted to cuss and scream at God for allowing it. But in the end I thanked God for giving me Stewie for the time he did. I told Stewie I loved him just as the Doc came through the door. They gave him the shot, and my Stewie was gone in the twinkle of an eye. I would have gladly taken the shot if it would have cured him. He not only saved my life more times than I can count, but he also taught me unconditional love.

Even now tears flow down my cheek as I write this. They are tears of joy and sorrow and a longing in my heart that I might hold him one more time. I love my family with everything I have and would die for them, but God used Stewie to bring me back to an understanding of what love was. We brought him home, burying him in the backyard. As I picked up the shovel, I told Deb I didn't want to do this. With tears rolling down my face, I dug the grave, and getting on my knees, I gently laid him in, covering him with soft dirt. Twice God used cats to keep me sober and from killing myself while teaching me things I needed to understand. Stewie was fifteen pounds of love and affection, and I will never forget him.

I wrote these three passages during some of my darkest days after we moved. They are a crying out to God for an acceptance of life on life's terms.

April 4, 2010

As the storms of life rage and tear at my being, my soul cries out with passion to be saved and made secure. The flesh tears at my members, driving me deeper and deeper into the valley of shadows. Tears spill down my face, and my body racks with sobs of despair. The joy I once knew and held dear is but a dream on the ash heap of selfish pride. The same one that led me to the pit of suicide and death now stands at the door once again. He has waited silently in the background for me. He has said, "I will have my vengeance on this one I once owned. When the time is ripe and his pride has been lifted up, I will cause him to fall, and I will be the victor. Though he hangs on with a thin gasp of faith, I will crush him and cause him to ever wonder. I will take the joy of his salvation and cause him to weep with despair, ever wondering if it is real. The end is worse than the beginning."

Take heed of where you stand in the darkness of this world. Though you belonged to the Lord, if you fail to follow him, he will let you have your way to the point of total despair. As you go down and death looks better than life, he is beside you waiting. His hand is stretched out for you to grasp as he raises you out of the slime of your existence. When you thought all was lost, he holds you in his arms, and you cling to him, asking for forgiveness.

You are embraced by his love, and he welcomes you back home. He sends someone to tell you that his grace is still upon you. The one that thinks he is untouchable is one waiting to fall. Walk in humility before God or you will fall in your pride.

April 5, 2010

A flood of tears rolls down the face of a sinner. Caught up in the throes of this world, I wonder why it is so painful. That which I sought has turned on me and rips my soul apart. The sweetness of the sin is no more. It rears its ugly head and thrashes about, tearing apart the very essence of all I held dear. The strength of my pride is turned into the weakness of my existence. That which I once sought has turned on me and crushed the very will to live from my members. I scream for relief, but it is not to be. Death looks so inviting and a quick escape from the pain. But even that is not to be. It is but a fleeting thought among millions that race through my mind.

May 8, 2010

Oh ye of little faith cast out doubt and walk in humility before the Spirit of the Lord.

This book tells bits of the path I took to becoming a full-blown alcoholic. It recounts some of the lives I touched and sometimes ruined on my way to insanity. It is not the full story but moments in time God had me place on paper. All people have a road they will travel, and the choices we make as we travel that road will determine how the end will be. Just as it was up to me to travel the road I chose, so it is with you.

I believe God had my life laid out before me as I was being formed in my mother's womb (Ps. 139:13-16 NKJV). It was not God who changed the plan but me when I chose to go down a different road than God had laid out for me. The reason I rebelled was because I wanted everything to be my way. I wanted to be in control. By His grace, the minute I ask for help the road converted to his road. There is hope for the alcoholic and drug addict. God can and will rescue us from ourselves if we search for him and then follow what people have done who were there before us. Is it easy? No, but it is only as hard as we make it.

I said before that God is not tolerant of sin, but you have to add:

1. Tolerance is the last virtue of a tolerant society.
2. The government is a reflection of its people. Where does that place us not only as a nation but also as individuals?

I wrote the following on December 26, 2012:

The great enlightenment of mankind is but a dim glow beheld from afar. There is no warmth to the glow, taking that which it has not earned and casting doubt as to what is real. It warms not the heart and makes desolate the sands of time.

Where will you go when your heart beats its last? If you think once you're dead it is over, I have one question: what if you are wrong? Just because you say there is no

God doesn't make it so. Are you that powerful? Every one of us is one heartbeat from eternity! The body we inhabit will one day die; of that we can be certain. We came from somewhere, and we most absolutely are going somewhere when we leave these bodies we have been using. Are you willing to take the chance that God does not exist? Remember, we are talking about where we are going to spend eternity, not what we want on our pizza.

There is nothing mystical that you have to do to accept Christ into your life. It is a simple prayer that can go something like this:

> Lord Jesus, I admit that I have sinned against you. I am sorry and ask for your forgiveness. Please come into my life and be my Lord and Savior. Amen.

God does not want our lives to be complicated, and he most certainly does not want the way to him to be complicated. Like I have said many times, it is not about religion but a relationship.

I have always told my children that the name on the door of the building is not important. Their doctrine must state that Jesus came to earth, born of a virgin woman, grew up, and at about the age of thirty started his ministry. For a three-year period, he preached that the kingdom of heaven was at hand. He did his ministry through the anointing of the Holy Spirit as a man even though he was God. At the end of three years, he was put to death on a cross, was buried in a tomb for three days, and then returned to life, eventually going home to be with Father God. He committed no sin while here on earth, dying sinless. It is only Jesus that we put our faith in for eternal salvation and none other. It is by grace (a free gift) and nothing else. You cannot be good enough to earn your salvation!

For my children:

I pray that my children will understand a little better why I reacted to life the way I did. I am so sorry for the way I was at times. Please forgive me for not showing love the way I should have. I wish I had been there more when I should have been, making more memories as a family. Spend time with your families and make lots of memories because that is the only thing you will take from this world. And above all, teach them about the love of Jesus while guiding them into a relationship with him.

For my wife:

Deb, other than Jesus, you have been my rock and my guide to areas of life I did not want to visit. I would not have done half the things I did if it had not been for you pushing me forward. You have made my life full. God blessed our union long before we stood in front of a minister. Please forgive me for the pain and hurt I caused you over the years, and the way you stuck with me is a testament to your strength. God has blessed me in many ways, but the greatest blessing has been you. I will forever love you, even during the times when you don't believe me.

Appendix

Matthew 25:42-43: for I was hungry and you gave Me no food; I was thirsty and you gave Me no drink, I was a stranger and you did not take me in, naked and you did not cloth Me, sick and in prison and you did not visit Me.

Psalm 139:7-12: Where can I go from your Spirit? Or where can I flee from your presence? If I ascend into heaven You are there; If I make my bed in hell, behold, You are there. If I take the wings of the morning, and dwell in the uttermost parts of the sea, Even there Your hand shall lead me, And your right hand shall hold me. If I say; "Surely the darkness shall fall on me," Even the night shall be light about me; Indeed, the darkness shall not hide from You, But the night shines as the day; The darkness and the light are both alike to You.

1 Corinthians 10:12-13: Therefore let him who thinks he stands take heed lest he fall. No temptation has overtaken you except such as is common to man; but God is faithful, who will not allow you to be tempted beyond what you are able, but with the temptation will also make the way of escape, that you may be able to bear it.

Psalm 53:1: The fool has said in his heart, "There is no God." They are corrupt, and have done abominable iniquity; There is none who does good.

Hebrews 13:8: Jesus Christ is the same yesterday, today, and forever.

Romans 9:18-21: Therefore he has mercy on whom He wills, and whom He will He hardens. You will say to me then, "Why does he still find fault? For who has resisted His will? But indeed, O man, who are you to reply against God? Will the thing formed say to him who formed it, "Why have you made me like this? Does not the potter have power over the clay, from the same lump to make one vessel for honor and another for dishonor?

2 Timothy 4:3-5: For the time will come when they will not endure sound doctrine, but according to their own desires, because they have itching ears, they will heap up for themselves teachers; and they will turn their ears away from the truth, and be turned aside to fables. But you be watch full in all things, endure afflictions, do the work of and evangelist, fulfill your ministry.

Matthew 6:19-21: Do not lay up for yourselves treasures on earth, where moth and rust destroy and where thieves break in and steal, but lay up for yourselves treasures in heaven, where neither moth nor rust destroys and where thieves do not break in and steal. For where your treasure is, there your heart will be also.

1 Thessalonians 5:16-18: Rejoice always, pray without ceasing, in everything give thanks; for this is the will of God in Christ Jesus for you.

Psalm 33:6-15: By the word of the Lord were the heavens made, their starry host by the breath of his mouth. He gathers the waters of the sea into jars, he puts the deep into storehouses. Let all the earth fear the Lord; all the people of the world revere him. For he spoke, and it came to be; he commanded, and it stood firm. The Lord foils the plans of the nations; he thwarts the purposes of the peoples. But the plans of the Lord stand firm forever, the purposes of his heart through all generations. Blessed is the nation whose God is the Lord, the people he chose for his inheritance. From heaven the Lord looks down and sees all mankind; from his dwelling place he watches all who live on earth—he who forms the hearts of all, who considers everything they do.

Matthew 8:19-20: Then a certain scribe came and said to Him, "Teacher, I will follow You wherever You go. And Jesus said to him, "Foxes have holes and birds of the air have nest, but the Son of Man has nowhere to lay his head.

Matthew 19:27-30: Then Peter answered and said to Him, "See, we have left all and followed You. Therefore what shall we have?" So Jesus said to them, "Assuredly I say to you, that in the regeneration, when the Son of Man sits on the throne of His glory, you who have followed Me will also sit on twelve thrones, judging the twelve tribes of Israel. And everyone who has left houses or brothers or sisters or father or mother or wife or children or lands, for My name's sake, shall receive a hundredfold, and inherit eternal life. But many who are first will be last, and the last first.

Matthew 5:14-16: You are the light of the world. A city that is set on a hill cannot be hidden. Nor do they light a lamp and put it under a basket, but on a lampstand and it gives light to all who are in the house. Let your light so shine before men, that they may see your good works and glorify your Father in heaven.

Romans 10:9-10: That if you confess with your mouth the Lord Jesus and believe in your heart that God has raised him from the dead, you will be saved. For with the heart one believes unto righteousness, and with the mouth confession is made unto salvation.

John 17:14-16: I have given them Your word; and the world has hated them because they are not of the world, just as I am not of the world. I do not pray that You should take them out of the world, but that You should keep them from the evil one. They are not of the world, just as I am not of the world.

Ephesians 5:18: And do not be drunk with wine, in which is dissipation; but be filled with the Spirit.

Psalm 139:13-16: For You formed my inward parts; You covered me in my mother's womb. I will praise You, for I am fearfully and wonderfully made; Marvelous Your works, And that my soul knows very well. My frame was not hidden from You, when I was made in secret, And skillfully wrought in the lowest parts of the earth. Your eyes saw my substance, being yet unformed. And in Your book they all were written, the days fashioned for me, when as yet there were none of them.

2 Corinthians 5:17: Therefore, if anyone is in Christ, he is a new creation; old things have passed away; behold, all things have become new.

Matthew 19:21: Jesus said to him, If you want to be perfect, go, sell what you have and give to the poor, and you will have treasure in heaven; and come, follow Me.

Romans 9:18-21: Therefore he has mercy on whom He wills, and whom He will He hardens. You will say to me then, "Why does he still find fault? For who has resisted His will? But indeed, O man, who are you to reply against God? Will the thing formed say to him who formed it, "Why have you made me like this? Does not the potter have power over the clay, from the same lump to make one vessel for honor and another for dishonor?

1 Corinthians 10:12-13: Therefore let him who thinks he stands take heed lest he fall. No temptation has overtaken you except such as is common to man; but God is faithful, who will not allow you to be tempted beyond what you are able, but with the temptation will also make the way of escape, that you may be able to bear it.

2 Timothy 4:3-5: For the time will come when they will not endure sound doctrine, but according to their own desires, because they have itching ears, they will heap up for themselves teachers; and they will turn their ears away from the truth, and be turned aside to fables. But you be watch full in all things, endure afflictions, do the work of and evangelist, fulfill your ministry

Works Cited

Pages 163-167 PTSD Symptoms taken from Veterans and Families Guide to Recovering from PTSD written by Stephanie Laite Lanham; 4th Edition 2007. Purple Heart Service Foundation, P.O. Box 49, Annandale, Va 22003

Pages 173-174 Treasures in Prison Cells by Bill Yount. Copyright 2013, Published By McDougal Publishing, P.O. Box 3595, Hagerstown, Md, 21742. Used with permission from Bill Yount.

53466431R00159

Made in the USA
Lexington, KY
06 July 2016